STYLE

BY
WALTER RALEIGH

STYLE

STYLE, the Latin name for an iron pen, has come to designate the art that handles, with ever fresh vitality and wary alacrity, the fluid elements of speech. By a figure, obvious enough, which yet might serve for an epitome of literary method, the most rigid and simplest of instruments has lent its name to the subtlest and most flexible of arts. Thence the application of the word has been extended to arts other than literature, to the whole range of the activities of man. The fact that we use the word "style" in speaking of architecture and sculpture, painting and music, dancing, play-acting, and cricket, that we can apply it to the careful achievements of the housebreaker and the poisoner, and to the spontaneous animal movements of the limbs of man or beast, is the noblest of p. 2unconscious tributes to the faculty of letters. The pen, scratching on wax or paper, has become the symbol of all that is expressive, all that is intimate, in human nature; not only arms and arts, but man himself, has yielded to it. His living voice, with its undulations and inflexions, assisted by the mobile play of feature and an infinite variety of bodily gesture, is driven to borrow dignity from the same metaphor; the orator and the actor are fain to be judged by style. "It is most true," says the author of *The Anatomy of Melancholy*, "*stylus virum arguit*, our style bewrays us." Other gestures shift and change and flit, this is the ultimate and enduring revelation of personality. The actor and the orator are condemned to work evanescent effects on transitory material; the dust that they write on is blown about their graves. The sculptor and the architect deal in less perishable ware, but the stuff is recalcitrant and stubborn, and will not take the impress of all states of the soul. Morals, philosophy, and æsthetic, mood and conviction, creed and whim, habit, passion, and demonstration—p. 3what art but the art of literature admits the entrance of all these, and guards them from the suddenness of mortality? What other art gives scope to natures and dispositions so diverse, and to tastes so contrarious? Euclid and Shelley, Edmund Spenser and Herbert Spencer, King David and David Hume, are all followers of the art of letters.

In the effort to explain the principles of an art so bewildering in its variety, writers on style have gladly availed themselves of analogy from the other arts, and have spoken, for the most part, not without a parable. It is a pleasant trick they put upon their pupils, whom they gladden with the delusion of a golden age, and perfection to be sought backwards, in arts less complex. The teacher of writing, past master in the juggling craft of language, explains that he is only carrying into letters the principles of counterpoint, or that it is all a matter of colour and perspective, or that structure and ornament are the beginning and end of his intent. Professor of eloquence and of thieving, his winged shoes remark him as he skips p. 4from metaphor to metaphor, not daring to trust himself to the partial and frail support of any single figure. He lures the astonished novice through as many trades as were ever housed in the central hall of the world's fair. From his distracting account of the business it would appear that he is now building a monument, anon he is painting a picture (with brushes dipped in a gallipot made of an earthquake); again he strikes a keynote, weaves a pattern, draws a wire, drives a nail, treads a measure, sounds a trumpet, or hits a target; or skirmishes around his subject; or lays it bare with a dissecting knife; or embalms a thought; or crucifies an enemy. What is he really doing all the time?

Besides the artist two things are to be considered in every art,—the instrument and the audience; or, to deal in less figured phrase, the medium and the public. From both of these the artist, if he would find freedom for the exercise of all his powers, must sit decently aloof. It is the misfortune of the actor, the singer, and the dancer, p. 5that their bodies are their sole instruments. On to the stage of their activities they carry the heart that nourishes them and the lungs wherewith they breathe, so that the soul, to escape degradation, must seek a more remote and difficult privacy. That immemorial right of the soul to make the body its home, a welcome escape from publicity and a refuge for sincerity, must be largely foregone by the actor, who has scant liberty to decorate and administer for his private behoof an apartment that is also a place of business. His ownership is limited by the necessities of his trade; when the customers are gone, he eats and sleeps in the bar-parlour. Nor is the instrument of his performances a thing of his choice; the poorest skill of the violinist may exercise itself upon a Stradivarius, but the actor is reduced to fiddle for the term of his natural life upon the face and fingers that he got from his mother. The serene detachment that may be achieved by disciples of greater arts can hardly be his, applause touches his personal pride too nearly, the mocking echoes of derision infest the solitude of his retired imagination. p. 6In none of the world's great polities has the practice of this art been found consistent with noble rank or honourable estate. Christianity might be expected to spare some sympathy for a calling that offers prizes to abandonment and self-immolation, but her eye is fixed on a more distant mark than the pleasure of the populace, and, as in gladiatorial Rome of old, her best efforts have been used to stop the games. Society, on the other hand, preoccupied with the art of life, has no warmer gift than patronage for those whose skill and energy exhaust themselves on the mimicry of life. The reward of social consideration is refused, it is true, to all artists, or accepted by them at their immediate peril. By a natural adjustment, in countries where the artist has sought and attained a certain modest social elevation, the issue has been changed, and the architect or painter, when his health is proposed, finds himself, sorely against the grain, returning thanks for the employer of labour, the genial host, the faithful husband, the tender father, and other pillars of society. The risk of toop. 7great familiarity with an audience which insists on honouring the artist irrelevantly, at the expense of the art, must be run by all; a more clinging evil besets the actor, in that he can at no time wholly escape from his phantasmal second self. On this creature of his art he has lavished the last doit of human capacity for expression; with what bearing shall he face the exacting realities of life? Devotion to his profession has beggared him of his personality; ague, old age and poverty, love and death, find in him an entertainer who plies them with a feeble repetition of the triumphs formerly prepared for a larger and less imperious audience. The very journalist—though he, too, when his profession takes him by the throat, may expound himself to his wife in phrases stolen from his own leaders—is a miracle of detachment in comparison; he has not put his laughter to sale. It is well for the soul's health of the artist that a definite boundary should separate his garden from his farm, so that when he escapes from the conventions that rule his work he may be free to recreate himself. But p. 8where shall the weary player keep holiday? Is not all the world a stage?

Whatever the chosen instrument of an art may be, its appeal to those whose attention it bespeaks must be made through the senses. Music, which works with the vibrations of a material substance, makes this appeal through the ear; painting through the eye; it is of a piece with the complexity of the literary art that it employs both channels,—as it might seem to a careless apprehension, indifferently.

For the writer's pianoforte is the dictionary, words are the material in which he works, and words may either strike the ear or be gathered by the eye from the printed page. The alternative will be called delusive, for, in European literature at least, there is no word-symbol that does not imply a spoken sound, and no excellence without euphony. But the other way is possible, the gulf between mind and mind may be bridged by something which has a right to the name of literature although it exacts no aid from the ear. The picture-writing of the Indians, the hieroglyphs p. 9of Egypt, may be cited as examples of literary meaning conveyed with no implicit help from the spoken word. Such an art, were it capable of high development, would forsake the kinship of melody, and depend for its sensual elements of delight on the laws of decorative pattern. In a land of deaf-mutes it might come to a measure of perfection. But where human intercourse is chiefly by speech, its connexion with the interests and passions of daily life would perforce be of the feeblest, it would tend more and more to cast off the fetters of meaning that it might do freer service to the jealous god of visible beauty. The overpowering rivalry of speech would rob it of all its symbolic intent and leave its bare picture. Literature has favoured rather the way of the ear and has given itself zealously to the tuneful ordering of sounds. Let it be repeated, therefore, that for the traffic of letters the senses are but the door-keepers of the mind; none of them commands an only way of access,—the deaf can read by sight, the blind by touch. It is not amid the bustle of the live senses, but in p. 10an under-world of dead impressions that Poetry works her will, raising that in power which was sown in weakness, quickening a spiritual body from the ashes of the natural body. The mind of man is peopled, like some silent city, with a sleeping company of reminiscences, associations, impressions, attitudes, emotions, to be awakened into fierce activity at the touch of words. By one way or another, with a fanfaronnade of the marching trumpets, or stealthily, by noiseless passages and dark posterns, the troop of suggesters enters the citadel, to do its work within. The procession of beautiful sounds that is a poem passes in through the main gate, and forthwith the by-ways resound to the hurry of ghostly feet, until the small company of adventurers is well-nigh lost and overwhelmed in that throng of insurgent spirits.

To attempt to reduce the art of literature to its component sense-elements is therefore vain. Memory, "the warder of the brain," is a fickle trustee, whimsically lavish to strangers, giving up to the appeal of a spoken word or unspoken p. 11symbol, an odour or a touch, all that has been garnered by the sensitive capacities of man. It is the part of the writer to play upon memory, confusing what belongs to one sense with what belongs to another, extorting images of colour at a word, raising ideas of harmony without breaking the stillness of the air. He can lead on the dance of words till their sinuous movements call forth, as if by mesmerism, the likeness of some adamantine rigidity, time is converted into space, and music begets sculpture. To see for the sake of seeing, to hear for the sake of hearing, are subsidiary exercises of his complex metaphysical art, to be counted among its rudiments. Picture and music can furnish but the faint beginnings of a philosophy of letters. Necessary though they be to a writer, they are transmuted in his service to new forms, and made to further purposes not their own.

The power of vision—hardly can a writer, least of all if he be a poet, forego that part of his equipment. In dealing with the impalpable, dim subjects that lie beyond the border-land of exact p. 12knowledge, the poetic instinct seeks always to bring them into clear definition and bright concrete imagery, so that it might seem for the moment as if painting also could deal with them. Every abstract conception, as it passes into the light of the creative imagination, acquires structure and firmness and colour, as flowers do in the light of the sun. Life and Death, Love and Youth, Hope and Time, become persons in poetry, not that they may wear the tawdry habiliments of the studio, but because persons are the objects of the most familiar sympathy and the most intimate knowledge.

How long, O Death? And shall thy feet depart
   Still a young child's with mine, or wilt thou stand
Full grown the helpful daughter of my heart,
   What time with thee indeed I reach the strand
Of the pale wave which knows thee what thou art,
   And drink it in the hollow of thy hand?

And as a keen eye for the imagery attendant on a word is essential to all writing, whether prose or poetry, that attempts the heart, so languor of the visual faculty can work disaster even in the calm periods of philosophic expatiation. "It p. 13cannot be doubted," says one whose daily meditations enrich *The People's Post-Bag*, "that Fear is, to a great extent, the mother of Cruelty." Alas, by the introduction of that brief proviso, conceived in a spirit of admirably cautious self-defence, the writer has unwittingly given himself to the horns of a dilemma whose ferocity nothing can mitigate. These tempered and conditional truths are not in nature, which decrees, with uncompromising dogmatism, that either a woman is one's mother, or she is not. The writer probably meant merely that "fear is one of the causes of cruelty," and had he used a colourless abstract word the platitude might pass unchallenged. But a vague desire for the emphasis and glamour of literature having brought in the word "mother," has yet failed to set the sluggish imagination to work, and a word so glowing with picture and vivid with sentiment is damped and dulled by the thumb-mark of besotted usage to mean no more than "cause" or "occasion." Only for the poet, perhaps, are words live winged things, flashing with colour and laden with scent; yet one poor _{p. 14}spark of imagination might save them from this sad descent to sterility and darkness.

Of no less import is the power of melody which chooses, rejects, and orders words for the satisfaction that a cunningly varied return of sound can give to the ear. Some critics have amused themselves with the hope that here, in the laws and practices regulating the audible cadence of words, may be found the first principles of style, the form which fashions the matter, the apprenticeship to beauty which alone can make an art of truth. And it may be admitted that verse, owning, as it does, a professed and canonical allegiance to music, sometimes carries its devotion so far that thought swoons into melody, and the thing said seems a discovery made by the way in the search for tuneful expression.

> What thing unto mine ear
> Wouldst thou convey,—what secret thing,
> O wandering water ever whispering?
> Surely thy speech shall be of her,
> Thou water, O thou whispering wanderer,
> What message dost thou bring?

In this stanza an exquisitely modulated tune p. 15is played upon the syllables that make up the word "wandering," even as, in the poem from which it is taken, there is every echo of the noise of waters laughing in sunny brooks, or moaning in dumb hidden caverns. Yet even here it would be vain to seek for reason why each particular sound of every line should be itself and no other. For melody holds no absolute dominion over either verse or prose; its laws, never to be disregarded, prohibit rather than prescribe. Beyond the simple ordinances that determine the place of the rhyme in verse, and the average number of syllables, or rhythmical beats, that occur in the line, where shall laws be found to regulate the sequence of consonants and vowels from syllable to syllable? Those few artificial restrictions, which verse invents for itself, once agreed on, a necessary and perilous license makes up the rest of the code. Literature can never conform to the dictates of pure euphony, while grammar, which has been shaped not in the interests of prosody, but for the service of thought, bars the way with its clumsy inalterable polysyllables and p. 16the monotonous sing-song of its inflexions. On the other hand, among a hundred ways of saying a thing, there are more than ninety that a care for euphony may reasonably forbid. All who have consciously practised the art of writing know what endless and painful vigilance is needed for the avoidance of the unfit or untuneful phrase, how the meaning must be tossed from expression to expression, mutilated and deceived, ere it can find rest in words. The stupid accidental recurrence of a single broad vowel; the cumbrous repetition of a particle; the emphatic phrase for which no emphatic place can be found without disorganising the structure of the period; the pert intrusion on a solemn thought of a flight of short syllables, twittering like a flock of sparrows; or that vicious trick of sentences whereby each, unmindful of its position and duties, tends to imitate the deformities of its predecessor;—these are a select few of the difficulties that the nature of language and of man conspire to put upon the writer. He is well served by his mind and ear if he can win past all p. 17such traps and ambuscades, robbed of only a little of his treasure, indemnified by the careless generosity of his spoilers, and still singing.

Besides their chime in the ear, and the images that they put before the mind's eye, words have, for their last and greatest possession, a meaning. They carry messages and suggestions that, in the effect wrought, elude all the senses equally. For the sake of this, their prime office, the rest is many times forgotten or scorned, the tune is disordered and havoc played with the lineaments of the picture, because without these the word can still do its business. The refutation of those critics who, in their analysis of the power of literature, make much of music and picture, is contained in the most moving passages that have found utterance from man. Consider the intensity of a saying like that of St. Paul:—"For I am persuaded, that neither death, nor life, nor angels, nor principalities, nor powers, nor things present, nor things to come, nor height, nor depth, nor any other creature, shall be able to separate us from the love of God, which is in Christ Jesus our Lord."

p. 18Do these verses draw their power from a skilful arrangement of vowel and consonant? But they are quoted from a translation, and can be translated otherwise, well or ill or indifferently, without losing more than a little of their virtue. Do they impress the eye by opening before it a prospect of vast extent, peopled by vague shapes? On the contrary, the visual embodiment of the ideas suggested kills the sense of the passage, by lowering the cope of the starry heavens to the measure of a poplar-tree. Death and life, height and depth, are conceived by the apostle, and creation thrown in like a trinket, only that they may lend emphasis to the denial that is the soul of his purpose. Other arts can affirm, or seem to affirm, with all due wealth of circumstance and detail; they can heighten their affirmation by the modesty of reserve, the surprises of a studied brevity, and the erasure of all impertinence; literature alone can deny, and honour the denial with the last resources of a power that has the universe for its treasury. It is this negative capability of words, their privative force, whereby p. 19 they can impress the minds with a sense of "vacuity, darkness, solitude, and silence," that Burke celebrates in the fine treatise of his younger days. In such a phrase as "the angel of the Lord" language mocks the positive rivalry of the pictorial art, which can offer only the poor pretence of an equivalent in a young man painted with wings. But the difference between the two arts is even better marked in the matter of negative suggestion; it is instanced by Burke from the noble passage where Virgil describes the descent of Æneas and the Sibyl to the shades of the nether world. Here are amassed all "the images of a tremendous dignity" that the poet could forge from the sublime of denial. The two most famous lines are a procession of negatives:—

Ibant obscuri sola sub nocte per umbram,
Perque domos Ditis vacuas et inania regna.

Through hollow kingdoms, emptied of the day,
And dim, deserted courts where Dis bears sway,
    Night-foundered, and uncertain of the path,
Darkling they took their solitary way.

Here is the secret of some of the cardinal p. 20 effects of literature; strong epithets like "lonely," "supreme," "invisible," "eternal," "inexorable," with the substantives that belong to them, borrow their force from the vastness of what they deny. And not these alone, but many other words, less indebted to logic for the magnificence of reach that it can lend, bring before the mind no picture, but a dim emotional framework. Such words as "ominous," "fantastic," "attenuated," "bewildered," "justification," are atmospheric rather than pictorial; they infect the soul with the passion-laden air that rises from humanity. It is precisely in his dealings with words like these, "heated originally by the breath of others," that a poet's fine sense and knowledge most avail him. The company a word has kept, its history, faculties, and predilections, endear or discommend it to his instinct. How hardly will poetry consent to employ such words as "congratulation" or "philanthropist,"—words of good origin, but tainted by long immersion in fraudulent rejoicings and pallid, comfortable, theoretic loves. How eagerly will the poetic imagination seize on a word p. 21 like "control," which gives scope by its very vagueness, and is fettered by no partiality of association. All words, the weak and the strong, the definite and the vague, have their offices to perform in language, but the loftiest purposes of poetry are seldom served by those explicit hard words which, like tiresome explanatory persons, say all that they mean. Only in the focus and centre of man's knowledge is there place for the hammer-blows of affirmation, the rest is a flickering world of hints and half-lights, echoes and suggestions, to be come at in the dusk or not at all.

The combination of these powers in words, of song and image and meaning, has given us the supreme passages of our romantic poetry. In Shakespeare's work, especially, the union of vivid definite presentment with immense reach of metaphysical suggestion seems to intertwine the roots of the universe with the particular fact; tempting the mind to explore that other side of the idea presented to it, the side turned away from it, and held by something behind.

<p. 22>It will have blood; they say blood win have blood:
Stones have been known to move and trees to speak;
Augurs and understood relations have
By maggot-pies and choughs and rooks brought forth
The secret'st man of blood.

This meeting of concrete and abstract, of sense and thought, keeps the eye travelling along the utmost skyline of speculation, where the heavens are interfused with the earth. In short, the third and greatest virtue of words is no other than the virtue that belongs to the weapons of thought,—a deep, wide, questioning thought that discovers analogies and pierces behind things to a half-perceived unity of law and essence. In the employ of keen insight, high feeling, and deep thinking, language comes by its own; the prettinesses that may be imposed on a passive material are as nothing to the splendour and grace that transfigure even the meanest instrument when it is wielded by the energy of thinking purpose. The contempt that is cast, by the vulgar phrase, on "mere words" bears witness to the rarity of this serious consummation. Yet by words the world was shaped out of chaos, by words the <p. 23>Christian religion was established among mankind. Are these terrific engines fit play-things for the idle humours of a sick child?

And now it begins to be apparent that no adequate description of the art of language can be drawn from the technical terminology of the other arts, which, like proud debtors, would gladly pledge their substance to repay an obligation that they cannot disclaim. Let one more attempt to supply literature with a parallel be quoted from the works of a writer on style, whose high merit it is that he never loses sight, either in theory or in practice, of the fundamental conditions proper to the craft of letters. Robert Louis Stevenson, pondering words long and lovingly, was impressed by their crabbed individuality, and sought to elucidate the laws of their arrangement by a reference to the principles of architecture. "The sister arts," he says, "enjoy the use of a plastic and ductile material, like the modeller's clay; literature alone is condemned to work in mosaic with finite and quite rigid words. You have seen those blocks, dear to the nursery: <p. 24>this one a pillar, that a pediment, a third a window or a vase. It is with blocks of just such arbitrary size and figure that the literary architect is condemned to design the palace of his art. Nor is this all; for since these blocks or words are the acknowledged currency of our daily affairs, there are here possible none of those suppressions by which other arts obtain relief, continuity, and vigour: no hieroglyphic touch, no smoothed impasto, no inscrutable shadow, as in painting; no blank wall, as in architecture; but every word, phrase, sentence, and paragraph must move in a logical progression, and convey a definite conventional import."

It is an acute comparison, happily indicative of the morose angularity that words offer to whoso handles them, admirably insistent on the chief of the incommodities imposed upon the writer, the necessity, at all times and at all costs, to mean something. The boon of the recurring monotonous expanse, that an apprentice may fill, the breathing-space of restful mechanical repetition, are denied to the writer, who must needs shoulder p. 25 the hod himself, and lay on the mortar, in ever varying patterns, with his own trowel. This is indeed the ordeal of the master, the canker-worm of the penny-a-liner, who, poor fellow, means nothing, and spends his life in the vain effort to get words to do the same. But if in this respect architecture and literature are confessed to differ, there remains the likeness that Mr. Stevenson detects in the building materials of the two arts, those blocks of "arbitrary size and figure; finite and quite rigid." There is truth enough in the comparison to make it illuminative, but he would be a rash dialectician who should attempt to draw from it, by way of inference, a philosophy of letters. Words are piled on words, and bricks on bricks, but of the two you are invited to think words the more intractable. Truly, it was a man of letters who said it, avenging himself on his profession for the never-ending toil it imposed, by miscalling it, with grim pleasantry, the architecture of the nursery. Finite and quite rigid words are not, in any sense that holds good of bricks. They move and change, they wax and p. 26 wane, they wither and burgeon; from age to age, from place to place, from mouth to mouth, they are never at a stay. They take on colour, intensity, and vivacity from the infection of neighbourhood; the same word is of several shapes and diverse imports in one and the same sentence; they depend on the building that they compose for the very chemistry of the stuff that composes them. The same epithet is used in the phrases "a fine day" and "fine irony," in "fair trade" and "a fair goddess." Were different symbols to be invented for these sundry meanings the art of literature would perish. For words carry with them all the meanings they have worn, and the writer shall be judged by those that he selects for prominence in the train of his thought. A slight technical implication, a faint tinge of archaism, in the common turn of speech that you employ, and in a moment you have shaken off the mob that scours the rutted highway, and are addressing a select audience of ticket-holders with closed doors. A single natural phrase of peasant speech, a direct physical sense given to a word that genteel p. 27 parlance authorises readily enough in its metaphorical sense, and at a touch you have blown the roof off the drawing-room of the villa, and have set its obscure inhabitants wriggling in the unaccustomed sun. In choosing a sense for your words you choose also an audience for them.

To one word, then, there are many meanings, according as it falls in the sentence, according as its successive ties and associations are broken or renewed. And here, seeing that the stupidest of all possible meanings is very commonly the slang meaning, it will be well to treat briefly of slang. For slang, in the looser acceptation of the term, is of two kinds, differing, and indeed diametrically opposite, in origin and worth. Sometimes it is the technical diction that has perforce been coined to name the operations, incidents, and habits of some way of life that society despises or deliberately elects to disregard. This sort of slang, which often invents names for what would otherwise go nameless, is vivid, accurate, and necessary, an addition of wealth to the world's dictionaries and of compass to the world's p. 28range of thought. Society, mistily conscious of the sympathy that lightens in any habitual name, seems to have become aware, by one of those wonderful processes of chary instinct which serve the great, vulnerable, timid organism in lieu of a brain, that to accept of the pickpocket his names for the mysteries of his trade is to accept also a new moral stand-point and outlook on the question of property. For this reason, and by no special masonic precautions of his own, the pickpocket is allowed to keep the admirable devices of his nomenclature for the familiar uses of himself and his mates, until a Villon arrives to prove that this language, too, was awaiting the advent of its bully and master. In the meantime, what directness and modest sufficiency of utterance distinguishes the dock compared with the fumbling prolixity of the old gentleman on the bench! It is the trite story,—romanticism forced to plead at the bar of classicism fallen into its dotage, Keats judged by *Blackwood*, Wordsworth exciting the pained astonishment of Miss Anna Seward. Accuser and accused alike recognise that a question of diction p. 29is part of the issue between them; hence the picturesque confession of the culprit, made in proud humility, that he "clicked a red 'un" must needs be interpreted, to save the good faith of the court, into the vaguer and more general speech of the classic convention. Those who dislike to have their watches stolen find that the poorest language of common life will serve their simple turn, without the rich technical additions of a vocabulary that has grown around an art. They can abide no rendering of the fact that does not harp incessantly on the disapproval of watch-owners. They carry their point of morals at the cost of foregoing all glitter and finish in the matter of expression.

This sort of slang, therefore, technical in origin, the natural efflorescence of highly cultivated agilities of brain, and hand, and eye, is worthy of all commendation. But there is another kind that goes under the name of slang, the offspring rather of mental sloth, and current chiefly among those idle, jocular classes to whom all art is a bugbear and a puzzle. There is a public for every p. 30one; the pottle-headed lout who in a moment of exuberance strikes on a new sordid metaphor for any incident in the beaten round of drunkenness, lubricity, and debt, can set his fancy rolling through the music-halls, and thence into the street, secure of applause and a numerous sodden discipleship. Of the same lazy stamp, albeit more amiable in effect, are the thought-saying contrivances whereby one word is retained to do the work of many. For the language of social intercourse ease is the first requisite; the average talker, who would be hard put to it if he were called on to describe or to define, must constantly be furnished with the materials of emphasis, wherewith to drive home his likes and dislikes. Why should he alienate himself from the sympathy of his fellows by affecting a singularity in the expression of his emotions? What he craves is not accuracy, but immediacy of expression, lest the tide of talk should flow past him, leaving him engaged in a belated analysis. Thus the word of the day is on all lips, and what was "vastly fine" last century is "awfully jolly" now; the meaning p. 31 is the same, the expression equally inappropriate. Oaths have their brief periods of ascendency, and philology can boast its fashion-plates. The tyrant Fashion, who wields for whip the fear of solitude, is shepherd to the flock of common talkers, as they run hither and thither pursuing, not self-expression, the prize of letters, but unanimity and self-obliteration, the marks of good breeding. Like those famous modern poets who are censured by the author of *Paradise Lost*, the talkers of slang are "carried away by custom, to express many things otherwise, and for the most part worse than else they would have exprest them." The poverty of their vocabulary makes appeal to the brotherly sympathy of a partial and like-minded auditor, who can fill out their paltry conventional sketches from his own experience of the same events. Within the limits of a single school, or workshop, or social circle, slang may serve; just as, between friends, silence may do the work of talk. There are few families, or groups of familiars, that have not some small coinage of this token-money, issued and accepted p. 32 by affection, passing current only within those narrow and privileged boundaries. This wealth is of no avail to the travelling mind, save as a memorial of home, nor is its material such "as, buried once, men want dug up again." A few happy words and phrases, promoted, for some accidental fitness, to the wider world of letters, are all that reach posterity; the rest pass into oblivion with the other perishables of the age.

A profusion of words used in an ephemeral slang sense is evidence, then, that the writer addresses himself merely to the uneducated and thoughtless of his own day; the revival of bygone meanings, on the other hand, and an archaic turn given to language is the mark rather of authors who are ambitious of a hearing from more than one age. The accretions of time bring round a word many reputable meanings, of which the oldest is like to be the deepest in grain. It is a counsel of perfection—some will say, of vainglorious pedantry—but that shaft flies furthest which is drawn to the head, and he who desires to be understood in the twenty-fourth century will p. 33 not be careless of the meanings that his words inherit from the fourteenth. To know them is of service, if only for the piquancy of avoiding them. But many times they cannot wisely be avoided, and the auspices under which a word began its career when first it was imported from the French or Latin overshadow it and haunt it to the end.

Popular modern usage will often rob common words, like "nice," "quaint," or "silly," of all flavour of their origin, as if it were of no moment to remember that these three words, at the outset of their history, bore the older senses of "ignorant," "noted," and "blessed." It may be granted that any attempt to return to these older senses, regardless of later implications, is stark pedantry; but a delicate writer will play shyly with the primitive significance in passing, approaching it and circling it, taking it as a point of reference or departure. The early faith of Christianity, its beautiful cult of childhood, and its appeal to unlearned simplicity, have left their mark on the meaning of "silly"; the history of the word is contained in that p. 34cry of St. Augustine, *Indocti surgunt et rapiunt coelum*, or in the fervent sentence of the author of the *Imitation*, *Oportet fieri stultum*. And if there is a later silliness, altogether unblest, the skilful artificer of words, while accepting this last extension, will show himself conscious of his paradox. So also he will shun the grossness that employs the epithet "quaint" to put upon subtlety and the devices of a studied workmanship an imputation of eccentricity; or, if he falls in with the populace in this regard, he will be careful to justify his innuendo. The slipshod use of "nice" to connote any sort of pleasurable emotion he will take care, in his writings at least, utterly to abhor. From the daintiness of elegance to the arrogant disgust of folly the word carries meanings numerous and diverse enough; it must not be cruelly burdened with all the laudatory occasions of an undiscriminating egotism.

It would be easy to cite a hundred other words like these, saved only by their nobler uses in literature from ultimate defacement. The higher standard imposed upon the written word tends to p. 35raise and purify speech also, and since talkers owe the same debt to writers of prose that these, for their part, owe to poets, it is the poets who must be accounted chief protectors, in the last resort, of our common inheritance. Every page of the works of that great exemplar of diction, Milton, is crowded with examples of felicitous and exquisite meaning given to the infallible word. Sometimes he accepts the secondary and more usual meaning of a word only to enrich it by the interweaving of the primary and etymological meaning. Thus the seraph Abdiel, in the passage that narrates his offer of combat to Satan, is said to "explore" his own undaunted heart, and there is no sense of "explore" that does not heighten the description and help the thought. Thus again, when the poet describes those

Eremites   and   friars,
White, Black, and Gray, with all their trumpery,

who inhabit, or are doomed to inhabit, the Paradise of Fools, he seems to invite the curious reader to recall the derivation of "trumpery," and so supplement the idea of worthlessness with that other p. 36idea, equally grateful to the author, of deceit. The strength that extracts this multiplex resonance of meaning from a single note is matched by the grace that gives to Latin words like "secure," "arrive," "obsequious," "redound," "infest," and "solemn" the fine precision of intent that art can borrow from scholarship.

Such an exactitude is consistent with vital change; Milton himself is bold to write "stood praying" for "continued kneeling in prayer," and deft to transfer the application of "schism" from the rent garment of the Church to those necessary "dissections made in the quarry and in the timber ere the house of God can be built." Words may safely veer to every wind that blows, so they keep within hail of their cardinal meanings, and drift not beyond the scope of their central employ, but when once they lose hold of that, then, indeed, the anchor has begun to drag, and the beach-comber may expect his harvest.

Fixity in the midst of change, fluctuation at the heart of sameness, such is the estate of language. According as they endeavour to reduce p. 37letters to some large haven and abiding-place of civility, or prefer to throw in their lot with the centrifugal tendency and ride on the flying crest of change, are writers dubbed Classic or Romantic. The Romantics are individualist, anarchic; the strains of their passionate incantation raise no cities to confront the wilderness in guarded symmetry, but rather bring the stars shooting from their spheres, and draw wild things captive to a voice. To them Society and Law seem dull phantoms, by the light cast from a flaming soul. They dwell apart, and torture their lives in the effort to attain to self-expression. All means and modes offered them by language they seize on greedily, and shape them to this one end; they ransack the vocabulary of new sciences, and appropriate or invent strange jargons. They furbish up old words or weld together new indifferently, that they may possess the machinery of their speech and not be possessed by it. They are at odds with the idiom of their country in that it serves the common need, and hunt it through all its metamorphoses to subject it to their private will. p. 38Heretics by profession, they are everywhere opposed to the party of the Classics, who move by slower ways to ends less personal, but in no wise easier of attainment. The magnanimity of the Classic ideal has had scant justice done to it by modern criticism. To make literature the crowning symbol of a world-wide civilisation; to roof in the ages, and unite the elect of all time in the courtesy of one shining assembly, paying duty to one unquestioned code; to undo the work of Babel, and knit together in a single community the scattered efforts of mankind towards order and reason;—this was surely an aim worthy of labour and sacrifice. Both have been freely given, and the end is yet to seek. The self-assertion of the recusants has found eulogists in plenty, but who has celebrated the self-denial that was thrown away on this other task, which is farther from fulfilment now than it was when the scholars of the Renaissance gave up their patriotism and the tongue of their childhood in the name of fellow-citizenship with the ancients and the œcumenical authority of letters? Scholars, grammarians, wits, and poets were content to bury p. 39the lustre of their wisdom and the hard-won fruits of their toil in the winding-sheet of a dead language, that they might be numbered with the family of Cicero, and added to the pious train of Virgil. It was a noble illusion, doomed to failure, the versatile genius of language cried out against the monotony of their Utopia, and the crowds who were to people the unbuilded city of their dreams went straying after the feathered chiefs of the rebels, who, when the fulness of time was come, themselves received apotheosis and the honours of a new motley pantheon. The tomb of that great vision bears for epitaph the ironical inscription which defines a Classic poet as "a dead Romantic."

In truth the Romantics are right, and the serenity of the classic ideal is the serenity of paralysis and death. A universal agreement in the use of words facilitates communication, but, so inextricably is expression entangled with feeling, it leaves nothing to communicate. Inanity dogs the footsteps of the classic tradition, which is everywhere lackeyed, through a long decline, by the pallor of reflected glories. Even the irresistible novelty p. 40of personal experience is dulled by being cast in the old matrix, and the man who professes to find the whole of himself in the Bible or in Shakespeare had as good not be. He is a replica and a shadow, a foolish libel on his Creator, who, from the beginning of time, was never guilty of tautology. This is the error of the classical creed, to imagine that in a fleeting world, where the quickest eye can never see the same thing twice, and a deed once done can never be repeated, language alone should be capable of fixity and finality. Nature avenges herself on those who would thus make her prisoner, their truths degenerate to truisms, and feeling dies in the ice-palaces that they build to house it. In their search for permanence they become unreal, abstract, didactic, lovers of generalisation, cherishers of the dry bones of life; their art is transformed into a science, their expression into an academic terminology. Immutability is their ideal, and they find it in the arms of death. Words must change to live, and a word once fixed becomes useless for the purposes of art. Whosoever p. 41would make acquaintance with the goal towards which the classic practice tends, should seek it in the vocabulary of the Sciences. There words are fixed and dead, a botanical collection of colourless, scentless, dried weeds, a *hortus siccus* of proper names, each individual symbol poorly tethered to some single object or idea. No wind blows through that garden, and no sun shines on it, to discompose the melancholy workers at their task of tying Latin labels on to withered sticks. Definition and division are the watchwords of science, where art is all for composition and creation. Not that the exact definable sense of a word is of no value to the stylist; he profits by it as a painter profits by a study of anatomy, or an architect by a knowledge of the strains and stresses that may be put on his material. The exact logical definition is often necessary for the structure of his thought and the ordering of his severer argument. But often, too, it is the merest beginning; when a word is once defined he overlays it with fresh associations and buries it under new-found moral significances, which may p. 42belie the definition they conceal. This is the burden of Jeremy Bentham's quarrel with "question-begging appellatives." A clear-sighted and scrupulously veracious philosopher, abettor of the age of reason, apostle of utility, god-father of the panopticon, and donor to the English dictionary of such unimpassioned vocables as "codification" and "international," Bentham would have been glad to purify the language by purging it of those "affections of the soul" wherein Burke had found its highest glory. Yet in censuring the ordinary political usage of such a word as "innovation," it was hardly prejudice in general that he attacked, but the particular and deep-seated prejudice against novelty. The surprising vivacity of many of his own figures,—although he had the courage of his convictions, and laboured, throughout the course of a long life, to desiccate his style,—bears witness to a natural skill in the use of loaded weapons. He will pack his text with grave argument on matters ecclesiastical, and indulge himself and literature, in the notes with a pleasant description of the flesh and p. 43the spirit playing leap-frog, now one up, now the other, around the holy precincts of the Church. Lapses like these show him far enough from his own ideal of a geometric fixity in the use of words. The claim of reason and logic to enslave language has a more modern advocate in the philosopher who denies all utility to a word while it retains traces of its primary sensuous employ. The tickling of the senses, the raising of the passions, these things do indeed interfere with the arid business of definition. None the less they are the life's breath of literature, and he is a poor stylist who cannot beg half-a-dozen questions in a single epithet, or state the conclusion he would fain avoid in terms that startle the senses into clamorous revolt.

The two main processes of change in words are Distinction and Assimilation. Endless fresh distinction, to match the infinite complexity of things, is the concern of the writer, who spends all his skill on the endeavour to cloth the delicacies of perception and thought with a neatly fitting garment. So words grow and bifurcate, diverge and dwindle, until one root has many branches. p. 44Grammarians tell how "royal" and "regal" grew up by the side of "kingly," how "hospital," "hospice," "hostel" and "hotel" have come by their several offices. The inventor of the word "sensuous" gave to the English people an opportunity of reconsidering those headstrong moral preoccupations which had already ruined the meaning of "sensual" for the gentler uses of a poet. Not only the Puritan spirit, but every special bias or interest of man seizes on words to appropriate them to itself. Practical men of business transfer such words as "debenture" or "commodity" from debt or comfort in general to the palpable concrete symbols of debt or comfort; and in like manlier doctors, soldiers, lawyers, shipmen,—all whose interest and knowledge are centred on some particular craft or profession, drag words from the general store and adapt them to special uses. Such words are sometimes reclaimed from their partial applications by the authority of men of letters, and pass back into their wider meanings enhanced by a new element of graphic association. Language never suffers p. 45by answering to an intelligent demand; it is indebted not only to great authors, but to all whom any special skill or taste has qualified to handle it. The good writer may be one who disclaims all literary pretension, but there he is, at work among words,—binding the vagabond or liberating the prisoner, exalting the humble or abashing the presumptuous, incessantly alert to amend their implications, break their lazy habits, and help them to refinement or scope or decision. He educates words, for he knows that they are alive.

Compare now the case of the ruder multitude. In the regard of literature, as a great critic long ago remarked, "all are the multitude; only they differ in clothes, not in judgment or understanding," p. 46and the poorest talkers do not inhabit the slums. Wherever thought and taste have fallen to be menials, there the vulgar dwell. How should they gain mastery over language? They are introduced to a vocabulary of some hundred thousand words, which quiver through a million of meanings; the wealth is theirs for the taking, and they are encouraged to be spendthrift by the very excess of what they inherit. The resources of the tongue they speak are subtler and more various than ever their ideas can put to use. So begins the process of assimilation, the edge put upon words by the craftsman is blunted by the rough treatment of the confident booby, who is well pleased when out of many highly-tempered swords he has manufactured a single clumsy coulter. A dozen expressions to serve one slovenly meaning inflate him with the sense of luxury and pomp. "Vast," "huge," "immense," "gigantic," "enormous," "tremendous," "portentous," and such-like groups of words, lose all their variety of sense in a barren uniformity of low employ. The reign of this democracy annuls differences of status, and insults over differences of ability or disposition. Thus do synonyms, or many words ill applied to one purpose, begin to flourish, and, for a last indignity, dictionaries of synonyms.

Let the truth be said outright: there are no synonyms, and the same statement can never be repeated in a changed form of words. Where the p. 47ignorance of one writer has introduced an unnecessary word into the language, to fill a place already occupied, the quicker apprehension of others will fasten upon it, drag it apart from its fellows, and find new work for it to do. Where a dull eye sees nothing but sameness, the trained faculty of observation will discern a hundred differences worthy of scrupulous expression. The old foresters had different names for a buck during each successive year of its life, distinguishing the fawn from the pricket, the pricket from the sore, and so forth, as its age increased. Thus it is also in that illimitable but not trackless forest of moral distinctions. Language halts far behind the truth of things, and only a drowsy perception can fail to devise a use for some new implement of description. Every strange word that makes its way into a language spins for itself a web of usage and circumstance, relating itself from whatsoever centre to fresh points in the circumference. No two words ever coincide throughout their whole extent. If sometimes good writers are found adding epithet to epithet for the same quality, and name to name p. 48for the same thing, it is because they despair of capturing their meaning at a venture, and so practise to get near it by a maze of approximations. Or, it may be, the generous breadth of their purpose scorns the minuter differences of related terms, and includes all of one affinity, fearing only lest they be found too few and too weak to cover the ground effectively. Of this sort are the so-called synonyms of the Prayer-Book, wherein we "acknowledge and confess" the sins we are forbidden to "dissemble or cloke;" and the bead-roll of the lawyer, who huddles together "give, devise, and bequeath," lest the cunning of litigants should evade any single verb. The works of the poets yield still better instances. When Milton praises the *Virtuous Young Lady* of his sonnet in that the spleen of her detractors moves her only to "pity and ruth," it is not for the idle filling of the line that he joins the second of these nouns to the first. Rather he is careful to enlarge and intensify his meaning by drawing on the stores of two nations, the one civilised, the other barbarous; and ruth is a quality as much more p. 49 instinctive and elemental than pity as pitilessness is keener, harder, and more deliberate than the inborn savagery of ruthlessness.

It is not chiefly, however, for the purposes of this accumulated and varied emphasis that the need of synonyms is felt. There is no more curious problem in the philosophy of style than that afforded by the stubborn reluctance of writers, the good as well as the bad, to repeat a word or phrase. When the thing is, they may be willing to abide by the old rule and say the word, but when the thing repeats itself they will seldom allow the word to follow suit. A kind of interdict, not removed until the memory of the first occurrence has faded, lies on a once used word. The causes of this anxiety for a varied expression are manifold. Where there is merely a column to fill, poverty of thought drives the hackney author into an illicit fulness, until the trick of verbiage passes from his practice into his creed, and makes him the dupe of his own puppets. A commonplace book, a dictionary of synonyms, and another of phrase and fable equip him for his task; if he p. 50 be called upon to marshal his ideas on the question whether oysters breed typhoid, he will acquit himself voluminously, with only one allusion (it is a point of pride) to the oyster by name. He will compare the succulent bivalve to Pandora's box, and lament that it should harbour one of the direst of ills that flesh is heir to. He will find a paradox and an epigram in the notion that the darling of Apicius should suffer neglect under the frowns of Æsculapius. Question, hypothesis, lamentation, and platitude dance their allotted round and fill the ordained space, while Ignorance masquerades in the garb of criticism, and Folly proffers her ancient epilogue of chastened hope. When all is said, nothing is said; and Montaigne's *Que sçais-je*, besides being briefer and wittier, was infinitely more informing.

But we dwell too long with disease; the writer nourished on thought, whose nerves are braced and his loins girt to struggle with a real meaning, is not subject to these tympanies. He feels no idolatrous dread of repetition when the theme requires, it, and is urged by no necessity of concealing real p. 51 identity under a show of change. Nevertheless he, too, is hedged about by conditions that compel him, now and again, to resort to what seems a synonym. The chief of these is the indispensable law of euphony, which governs the sequence not only of words, but also of phrases. In proportion as a phrase is memorable, the words that compose it become mutually adhesive, losing for a time something of their individual scope, bringing with them, if they be torn away too quickly, some cumbrous fragments of their recent association. That he may avoid this, a sensitive writer is often put to his shifts, and extorts, if he be fortunate, a triumph from the accident of his encumbrance. By a slight stress laid on the difference of usage the unshapeliness may be done away with, and a new grace found where none was sought. Addison and Landor accuse Milton, with reason, of too great a fondness for the pun, yet surely there is something to please the mind, as well as the ear, in the description of the heavenly judgment,

That brought into this world a world of woe.

Where words are not fitted with a single hard p. 52definition, rigidly observed, all repetition is a kind of delicate punning, bringing slight differences of application into clear relief. The practice has its dangers for the weak-minded lover of ornament, yet even so it may be preferable to the flat stupidity of one identical intention for a word or phrase in twenty several contexts. For the law of incessant change is not so much a counsel of perfection to be held up before the apprentice, as a fundamental condition of all writing whatsoever; if the change be not ordered by art it will order itself in default of art. The same statement can never be repeated even in the same form of words, and it is not the old question that is propounded at the third time of asking. Repetition, that is to say, is the strongest generator of emphasis known to language. Take the exquisite repetitions in these few lines:—

Bitter constraint and sad occasion dear
Compels me to disturb your season due;
For Lycidas is dead, dead ere his prime,
Young Lycidas, and hath not left his peer.

Here the tenderness of affection returns again p. 53to the loved name, and the grief of the mourner repeats the word "dead." But this monotony of sorrow is the least part of the effect, which lies rather in the prominence given by either repetition to the most moving circumstance of all—the youthfulness of the dead poet. The attention of the discursive intellect, impatient of reiteration, is concentrated on the idea which these repeated and exhausted words throw into relief. Rhetoric is content to borrow force from simpler methods; a good orator will often bring his hammer down, at the end of successive periods, on the same phrase; and the mirthless refrain of a comic song, or the catchword of a buffoon, will raise laughter at last by its brazen importunity. Some modern writers, admiring the easy power of the device, have indulged themselves with too free a use of it; Matthew Arnold particularly, in his prose essays, falls to crying his text like a hawker,

> Beating it in upon our weary brains,
> As tho' it were the burden of a song,

clattering upon the iron of the Philistine giant in the effort to bring him to reason. These are the p. 54 ostentatious violences of a missionary, who would fain save his enemy alive, where a grimmer purpose is glad to employ a more silent weapon and strike but once. The callousness of a thick-witted auditory lays the need for coarse method on the gentlest soul resolved to stir them. But he whose message is for minds attuned and tempered will beware of needless reiteration, as of the noisiest way of emphasis. Is the same word wanted again, he will examine carefully whether the altered incidence does not justify and require an altered term, which the world is quick to call a synonym. The right dictionary of synonyms would give the context of each variant in the usage of the best authors. To enumerate all the names applied by Milton to the hero of *Paradise Lost*, without reference to the passages in which they occur, would be a foolish labour; with such reference, the task is made a sovereign lesson in style. At Hell gates, where he dallies in speech with his leman Sin to gain a passage from the lower World, Satan is "the subtle Fiend," in the garden of Paradise he is "the Tempter" and "the Enemy of Mankind," p. 55 putting his fraud upon Eve he is the "wily Adder," leading her in full course to the tree he is "the dire Snake," springing to his natural height before the astonished gaze of the cherubs he is "the grisly King." Every fresh designation elaborates his character and history, emphasises the situation, and saves a sentence. So it is with all variable appellations of concrete objects; and even in the stricter and more conventional region of abstract ideas the same law runs. Let a word be changed or repeated, it brings in either case its contribution of emphasis, and must be carefully chosen for the part it is to play, lest it should upset the business of the piece by irrelevant clownage in the midst of high matter, saying more or less than is set down for it in the author's purpose.

The chameleon quality of language may claim yet another illustration. Of origins we know nothing certainly, nor how words came by their meanings in the remote beginning, when speech, like the barnacle-goose of the herbalist, was suspended over an expectant world, ripening on a tree. But this we know, that language in its p. 56 mature state is fed and fattened on metaphor. Figure is not a late device of the rhetorician, but the earliest principle of change in language. The whole process of speech is a long series of exhilarating discoveries, whereby words, freed from the swaddling bands of their nativity, are found capable of new relations and a wider metaphorical employ. Then, with the growth of exact knowledge, the straggling associations that attended the word on its travels are straitened and confined, its meaning is settled, adjusted, and balanced, that it may bear its part in the scrupulous deposition of truth. Many are the words that have run this double course, liberated from their first homely offices and transformed by poetry, reclaimed in a more abstract sense, and appropriated to a new set of facts by science. Yet a third chance awaits them when the poet, thirsty for novelty, passes by the old simple founts of figure to draw metaphor from the latest technical applications of specialised terms. Everywhere the intuition of poetry, impatient of the sturdy philosophic cripple that lags so p. 57far behind, is busy in advance to find likenesses not susceptible of scientific demonstration, to leap to comparisons that satisfy the heart while they leave the colder intellect only half convinced. When an elegant dilettante like Samuel Rogers is confronted with the principle of gravitation he gives voice to science in verse:—

That very law which moulds a tear,
    And bids it trickle from its source,
That law preserves the earth a sphere,
    And guides the planets in their course.

But a seer like Wordsworth will never be content to write tunes for a text-book of physics, he boldly confounds the arbitrary limits of matter and morals in one splendid apostrophe to Duty:—

Flowers laugh before thee on their beds;
    And fragrance in thy footing treads;
    Thou dost preserve the stars from wrong;
And the most ancient heavens, through thee, are fresh and strong.

Poets, it is said, anticipate science; here in these four lines is work for a thousand laboratories for a thousand years. But the truth has been understated; every writer and every speaker p. 58works ahead of science, expressing analogies and contrasts, likenesses and differences, that will not abide the apparatus of proof. The world of perception and will, of passion and belief, is an uncaptured virgin, airily deriding from afar the calculated advances and practised modesty of the old bawd Science; turning again to shower a benediction of unexpected caresses on the most cavalier of her wooers, Poetry. This world, the child of Sense and Faith, shy, wild, and provocative, for ever lures her lovers to the chase, and the record of their hopes and conquests is contained in the lover's language, made up wholly of parable and figure of speech. There is nothing under the sun nor beyond it that does not concern man, and it is the unceasing effort of humanity, whether by letters or by science, to bring "the commerce of the mind and of things" to terms of nearer correspondence. But Literature, ambitious to touch life on all its sides, distrusts the way of abstraction, and can hardly be brought to abandon the point of view whence things are seen in their immediate relation to the p. 59individual soul. This kind of research is the work of letters; here are facts of human life to be noted that are never like to be numerically tabulated, changes and developments that defy all metrical standards to be traced and described. The greater men of science have been cast in so generous a mould that they have recognised the partial nature of their task; they have known how to play with science as a pastime, and to win and wear her decorations for a holiday favour. They have not emaciated the fulness of their faculties in the name of certainty, nor cramped their humanity for the promise of a future good. They have been the servants of Nature, not the slaves of method. But the grammarian of the laboratory is often the victim of his trade. He staggers forth from his workshop, where prolonged concentration on a mechanical task, directed to a provisional and doubtful goal, has dimmed his faculties; the glaring motley of the world, bathed in sunlight, dazzles him; the questions, moral, political, and personal, that his method has relegated to some future of larger p. 60knowledge, crowd upon him, clamorous for solution, not to be denied, insisting on a settlement to-day. He is forced to make a choice, and may either forsake the divinity he serves, falling back, for the practical and æsthetic conduct of life, on those common instincts of sensuality which oscillate between the conventicle and the tavern as the poles of duty and pleasure, or, more pathetically still, he may attempt to bring the code of the observatory to bear immediately on the vagaries of the untameable world, and suffer the pedant's disaster. A martyr to the good that is to be, he has voluntarily maimed himself "for the kingdom of Heaven's sake"—if, perchance, the kingdom of Heaven might come by observation. The enthusiasm of his self-denial shows itself in his unavailing struggle to chain language also to the bare rock of ascertained fact. Metaphor, the poet's right-hand weapon, he despises; all that is tentative, individual, struck off at the urging of a mood, he disclaims and suspects. Yet the very rewards that science promises have their parallel in the domain of letters. The discovery of likeness p. 61in the midst of difference, and of difference in the midst of likeness, is the keenest pleasure of the intellect; and literary expression, as has been said, is one long series of such discoveries, each with its thrill of incommunicable happiness, all unprecedented, and perhaps unverifiable by later experiment. The finest instrument of these discoveries is metaphor, the spectroscope of letters.

Enough has been said of change; it remains to speak of one more of those illusions of fixity wherein writers seek exemption from the general lot. Language, it has been shown, is to be fitted to thought; and, further, there are no synonyms. What more natural conclusion could be drawn by the enthusiasm of the artist than that there is some kind of preordained harmony between words and things, whereby expression and thought tally exactly, like the halves of a puzzle? This illusion, called in France the doctrine of the *mot propre*, is a will o' the wisp which has kept many an artist dancing on its trail. That there is one, and only one way of expressing one thing has p. 62been the belief of other writers besides Gustave Flaubert, inspiriting them to a desperate and fruitful industry. It is an amiable fancy, like the dream of Michael Angelo, who loved to imagine that the statue existed already in the block of marble, and had only to be stripped of its superfluous wrappings, or like the indolent fallacy of those economic soothsayers to whom Malthus brought rough awakening, that population and the means of subsistence move side by side in harmonious progress.

But hunger does not imply food, and there may hover in the restless heads of poets, as themselves testify—

One thought, one grace, one wonder, at the least,
Which into words no virtue can digest.

Matter and form are not so separable as the popular philosophy would have them; indeed, the very antithesis between them is a cardinal instance of how language reacts on thought, modifying and fixing a cloudy truth. The idea pursues form not only that it may be known to others, but that it may know itself, and the body in which it becomes incarnate is not to be distinguished from p. 63the informing soul. It is recorded of a famous Latin historian how he declared that he would have made Pompey win the battle of Pharsalia had the effective turn of the sentence required it. He may stand for the true type of the literary artist. The business of letters, howsoever simple it may seem to those who think truth-telling a gift of nature, is in reality two-fold, to find words for a meaning, and to find a meaning for words. Now it is the words that refuse to yield, and now the meaning, so that he who attempts to wed them is at the same time altering his words to suit his meaning, and modifying and shaping his meaning to satisfy the requirements of his words. The humblest processes of thought have had their first education from language long before they took shape in literature. So subtle is the connexion between the two that it is equally possible to call language the form given to the matter of thought, or, inverting the application of the figure, to speak of thought as the formal principle that shapes the raw material of language. It is not until the two become one that they can be p. 64known for two. The idea to be expressed is a kind of mutual recognition between thought and language, which here meet and claim each other for the first time, just as in the first glance exchanged by lovers, the unborn child opens its eyes on the world, and pleads for life. But thought, although it may indulge itself with the fancy of a predestined affiance, is not confined to one mate, but roves free and is the father of many children. A belief in the inevitable word is the last refuge of that stubborn mechanical theory of the universe which has been slowly driven from science, politics, and history. Amidst so much that is undulating, it has pleased writers to imagine that truth persists and is provided by heavenly munificence with an imperishable garb of language. But this also is vanity, there is one end appointed alike to all, fact goes the way of fiction, and what is known is no more perdurable than what is made. Not words nor works, but only that which is formless endures, the vitality that is another name for change, the breath that fills and shatters the bubbles of good and p. 65evil, of beauty and deformity, of truth and untruth.

No art is easy, least of all the art of letters. Apply the musical analogy once more to the instrument whereon literature performs its voluntaries. With a living keyboard of notes which are all incessantly changing in value, so that what rang true under Dr. Johnson's hand may sound flat or sharp now, with a range of a myriad strings, some falling mute and others being added from day to day, with numberless permutations and combinations, each of which alters the tone and pitch of the units that compose it, with fluid ideas that never have an outlined existence until they have found their phrases and the improvisation is complete, is it to be wondered at that the art of style is eternally elusive, and that the attempt to reduce it to rule is the forlorn hope of academic infatuation?

These difficulties and complexities of the instrument are, nevertheless, the least part of the ordeal that is to be undergone by the writer. The p. 66same musical note or phrase affects different ears in much the same way; not so the word or group of words. The pure idea, let us say, is translated into language by the literary composer; who is to be responsible for the retranslation of the language into idea? Here begins the story of the troubles and weaknesses that are imposed upon literature by the necessity it lies under of addressing itself to an audience, by its liability to anticipate the corruptions that mar the understanding of the spoken or written word. A word is the operative symbol of a relation between two minds, and is chosen by the one not without regard to the quality of the effect actually produced upon the other. Men must be spoken to in their accustomed tongue, and persuaded that the unknown God proclaimed by the poet is one whom aforetime they ignorantly worshipped. The relation of great authors to the public may be compared to the war of the sexes, a quiet watchful antagonism between two parties mutually indispensable to each other, at one time veiling itself in endearments, at another breaking out into open p. 67defiance. He who has a message to deliver must wrestle with his fellows before he shall be permitted to ply them with uncomfortable or unfamiliar truths. The public, like the delicate Greek Narcissus, is sleepily enamoured of itself; and the name of its only other perfect lover is Echo. Yet even great authors must lay their account with the public, and it is instructive to observe how different are the attitudes they have adopted, how uniform the disappointment they have felt. Some, like Browning and Mr. Meredith in our own day, trouble themselves little about the reception given to their work, but are content to say on, until the few who care to listen have expounded them to the many, and they are applauded, in the end, by a generation whom they have trained to appreciate them. Yet this noble and persevering indifference is none of their choice, and long years of absolution from criticism must needs be paid for in faults of style. "Writing for the stage," Mr. Meredith himself has remarked, "would be a corrective of a too-incrusted scholarly style into which some great ones fall at times." Denied such a corrective, the p. 68great one is apt to sit alone and tease his meditations into strange shapes, fortifying himself against obscurity and neglect with the reflection that most of the words he uses are to be found, after all, in the dictionary. It is not, however, from the secluded scholar that the sharpest cry of pain is wrung by the indignities of his position, but rather from genius in the act of earning a full meed of popular applause. Both Shakespeare and Ben Jonson wrote for the stage, both were blown by the favouring breath of their plebeian patrons into reputation and a competence. Each of them passed through the thick of the fight, and well knew that ugly corner where the artist is exposed to cross fires, his own idea of masterly work on the one hand and the necessity for pleasing the rabble on the other. When any man is awake to the fact that the public is a vile patron, when he is conscious also that his bread and his fame are in their gift—it is a stern passage for his soul, a touchstone for the strength and gentleness of his spirit. Jonson, whose splendid scorn took to itself lyric wings in the two great Odes to Himself, sang p. 69high and aloof for a while, then the frenzy caught him, and he flung away his lyre to gird himself for deeds of mischief among nameless and noteless antagonists. Even Chapman, who, in *The Tears of Peace*, compares "men's refuse ears" to those gates in ancient cities which were opened only when the bodies of executed malefactors were to be cast away, who elsewhere gives utterance, in round terms, to his belief that

No   truth   of   excellence   was   ever   seen
But bore the venom of the vulgar's spleen,

—even the violences of this great and haughty spirit must pale beside the more desperate violences of the dramatist who commended his play to the public in the famous line,

By God, 'tis good, and if you like't, you may.

This stormy passion of arrogant independence disturbs the serenity of atmosphere necessary for creative art. A greater than Jonson donned the suppliant's robes, like Coriolanus, and with the inscrutable honeyed smile about his lips begged for the "most sweet voices" of the journeymen p. 70and gallants who thronged the Globe Theatre. Only once does the wail of anguish escape him—

Alas!   'tis   true,   I   have   gone   here   and   there,
    And   made   myself   a   motley   to   the   view,
Gored mine own thoughts, sold cheap what is most dear.

And again—

Thence   comes   it   that   my   name   receives   a   brand,
    And   almost   thence   my   nature   is   subdued
To   what   it   works   in,   like   the   dyer's   hand,
  Pity me then, and wish I were renewed.

Modern vulgarity, speaking through the mouths of Shakesperian commentators, is wont to interpret these lines as a protest against the contempt wherewith Elizabethan society regarded the professions of playwright and actor. We are asked to conceive that Shakespeare humbly desires the pity of his bosom friend because he is not put on the same level of social estimation with a brocaded gull or a prosperous stupid goldsmith of the Cheap. No, it is a cry, from the depth of his nature, for forgiveness because he has sacrificed a little on the altar of popularity. Jonson would p. 71 have boasted that he never made this sacrifice. But he lost the calm of his temper and the clearness of his singing voice, he degraded his magnanimity by allowing it to engage in street-brawls, and he endangered the sanctuary of the inviolable soul.

At least these great artists of the sixteenth and nineteenth centuries are agreed upon one thing, that the public, even in its most gracious mood, makes an ill task-master for the man of letters. It is worth the pains to ask why, and to attempt to show how much of an author's literary quality is involved in his attitude towards his audience. Such an inquiry will take us, it is true, into bad company, and exhibit the vicious, the fatuous, and the frivolous posturing to an admiring crowd. But style is a property of all written and printed matter, so that to track it to its causes and origins is a task wherein literary criticism may profit by the humbler aid of anthropological research.

Least of all authors is the poet subject to the tyranny of his audience. "Poetry and eloquence," p. 72 says John Stuart Mill, "are both alike the expression or utterance of feeling. But if we may be excused the antithesis, we should say that eloquence is heard, poetry is overheard. Eloquence supposes an audience; the peculiarity of poetry appears to us to lie in the poet's utter unconsciousness of a listener." Poetry, according to this discerning criticism, is an inspired soliloquy; the thoughts rise unforced and unchecked, taking musical form in obedience only to the law of their being, giving pleasure to an audience only as the mountain spring may chance to assuage the thirst of a passing traveller. In lyric poetry, language, from being a utensil, or a medium of traffic and barter, passes back to its place among natural sounds; its affinity is with the wind among the trees and the stream among the rocks; it is the cry of the heart, as simple as the breath we draw, and as little ordered with a view to applause. Yet speech grew up in society, and even in the most ecstatic of its uses may flag for lack of understanding and response. It were rash to say that the poets need no audience; the loneliest have p. 73 promised themselves a tardy recognition, and some among the greatest came to their maturity in the warm atmosphere of a congenial society. Indeed the ratification set upon merit by a living audience, fit though few, is necessary for the development of the most humane and sympathetic genius; and the memorable ages of literature, in Greece or Rome, in France or England, have been the ages of a literary society. The nursery of our greatest dramatists must be looked for, not, it is true, in the transfigured bear-gardens of the Bankside, but in those enchanted taverns, islanded and bastioned by the protective decree—

Idiota, insulsus, tristis, turpis, abesto.

The poet seems to be soliloquising because he is addressing himself, with the most entire confidence, to a small company of his friends, who may even, in unhappy seasons, prove to be the creatures of his imagination. Real or imaginary, they are taken by him for his equals; he expects from them a quick intelligence and a perfect sympathy, which may enable him to despise all p. 74concealment. He never preaches to them, nor scolds, nor enforces the obvious. Content that what he has spoken he has spoken, he places a magnificent trust on a single expression. He neither explains, nor falters, nor repents; he introduces his work with no preface, and cumbers it with no notes. He will not lower nor raise his voice for the sake of the profane and idle who may chance to stumble across his entertainment. His living auditors, unsolicited for the tribute of worship or an alms, find themselves conceived of in the likeness of what he would have them to be, raised to a companion pinnacle of friendship, and constituted peers and judges, if they will, of his achievement. Sometimes they come late.

This blend of dignity and intimacy, of candour and self-respect, is unintelligible to the vulgar, who understand by intimacy mutual concession to a base ideal, and who are so accustomed to deal with masks, that when they see a face they are shocked as by some grotesque. Now a poet, like Montaigne's naked philosopher, is all face; and the bewilderment of his masked and muffled critics p. 75is the greater. Wherever he attracts general attention he cannot but be misunderstood. The generality of modern men and women who pretend to literature are not hypocrites, or they might go near to divine him,—for hypocrisy, though rooted in cowardice, demands for its flourishing a clear intellectual atmosphere, a definite aim, and a certain detachment of the directing mind. But they are habituated to trim themselves by the cloudy mirror of opinion, and will mince and temporise, as if for an invisible audience, even in their bedrooms. Their masks have, for the most part, grown to their faces, so that, except in some rare animal paroxysm of emotion, it is hardly themselves that they express. The apparition of a poet disquiets them, for he clothes himself with the elements, and apologises to no idols. His candour frightens them: they avert their eyes from it; or they treat it as a licensed whim; or, with a sudden gleam of insight, and apprehension of what this means for them and theirs, they scream aloud for fear. A modern instance may be found in the angry protestations launched p. 76against Rossetti's Sonnets, at the time of their first appearance, by a writer who has since matched himself very exactly with an audience of his own kind. A stranger freak of burgess criticism is everyday fare in the odd world peopled by the biographers of Robert Burns. The nature of Burns, one would think, was simplicity itself; it could hardly puzzle a ploughman, and two sailors out of three would call him brother. But he lit up the whole of that nature by his marvellous genius for expression, and grave personages have been occupied ever since in discussing the dualism of his character, and professing to find some dark mystery in the existence of this, that, or the other trait—a love of pleasure, a hatred of shams, a deep sense of religion. It is common human nature, after all, that is the mystery, but they seem never to have met with it, and treat it as if it were the poet's eccentricity. They are all agog to worship him, and when they have made an image of him in their own likeness, and given it a tin-pot head that exactly hits their taste, they break into noisy lamentation over the discovery p. 77 that the original was human, and had feet of clay. They deem "Mary in Heaven" so admirable that they could find it in their hearts to regret that she was ever on earth. This sort of admirers constantly refuses to bear a part in any human relationship; they ask to be fawned on, or trodden on, by the poet while he is in life; when he is dead they make of him a candidate for godship, and heckle him. It is a misfortune not wholly without its compensations that most great poets are dead before they are popular.

If great and original literary artists—here grouped together under the title of poets—will not enter into transactions with their audience, there is no lack of authors who will. These are not necessarily charlatans; they may have by nature a ready sympathy with the grossness of the public taste, and thus take pleasure in studying to gratify it. But man loses not a little of himself in crowds, and some degradation there must be where the one adapts himself to the many. The British public is not seen at its best when it is enjoying a holiday in a foreign country, nor when p. 78 it is making excursions into the realm of imaginative literature: those who cater for it in these matters must either study its tastes or share them. Many readers bring the worst of themselves to a novel; they want lazy relaxation, or support for their nonsense, or escape from their creditors, or a free field for emotions that they dare not indulge in life. The reward of an author who meets them half-way in these respects, who neither puzzles nor distresses them, who asks nothing from them, but compliments them on their great possessions and sends them away rejoicing, is a full measure of acceptance, and editions unto seventy times seven.

The evils caused by the influence of the audience on the writer are many. First of all comes a fault far enough removed from the characteristic vices of the charlatan—to wit, sheer timidity and weakness. There is a kind of stage-fright that seizes on a man when he takes pen in hand to address an unknown body of hearers, no less than when he stands up to deliver himself to a sea of expectant faces. This is the true panic fear, that walks at mid-day, and p. 79 unmans those whom it visits. Hence come reservations, qualifications, verbosity, and the see-saw of a wavering courage, which apes progress and purpose, as soldiers mark time with their feet. The writing produced under these auspices is of no greater moment than the incoherent loquacity of a nervous patient. All self-expression is a challenge thrown down to the world, to be taken up by whoso will; and the spirit of timidity, when it touches a man, suborns him with the reminder that he holds his life and goods by the sufferance of his fellows. Thereupon he begins to doubt whether it is worth while to court a verdict of so grave possibilities, or to risk offending a judge—whose customary geniality is merely the outcome of a fixed habit of inattention. In doubt whether to speak or keep silence, he takes a middle course, and while purporting to speak for himself, is careful to lay stress only on the points whereon all are agreed, to enlarge eloquently on the doubtfulness of things, and to give to words the very least meaning that they will carry. Such a procedure, which glides over essentials, and handles truisms p. 80or trivialities with a fervour of conviction, has its functions in practice. It will win for a politician the coveted and deserved repute of a "safe" man—safe, even though the cause perish. Pleaders and advocates are sometimes driven into it, because to use vigorous, clean, crisp English in addressing an ordinary jury or committee is like flourishing a sword in a drawing-room: it will lose the case. Where the weakest are to be convinced speech must stoop: a full consideration of the velleities and uncertainties, a little bombast to elevate the feelings without committing the judgment, some vague effusion of sentiment, an inapposite blandness, a meaningless rodomontade—these are the by-ways to be travelled by the style that is a willing slave to its audience. The like is true of those documents—petitions, resolutions, congratulatory addresses, and so forth—that are written to be signed by a multitude of names. Public occasions of this kind, where all and sundry are to be satisfied, have given rise to a new parliamentary dialect, which has nothing of the freshness of individual emotion, is powerless to deal with p. 81realities, and lacks all resonance, vitality, and nerve. There is no cure for this, where the feelings and opinions of a crowd are to be expressed. But where indecision is the ruling passion of the individual, he may cease to write. Popularity was never yet the prize of those whose only care is to avoid offence.

For hardier aspirants, the two main entrances to popular favour are by the twin gates of laughter and tears. Pathos knits the soul and braces the nerves, humour purges the eyesight and vivifies the sympathies; the counterfeits of these qualities work the opposite effects. It is comparatively easy to appeal to passive emotions, to play upon the melting mood of a diffuse sensibility, or to encourage the narrow mind to dispense a patron's laughter from the vantage-ground of its own small preconceptions. Our annual crop of sentimentalists and mirth-makers supplies the reading public with food. Tragedy, which brings the naked soul face to face with the austere terrors of Fate, Comedy, which turns the light inward and dissipates the mists of self-affection and self-esteem, p. 82have long since given way on the public stage to the flattery of Melodrama, under many names. In the books he reads and in the plays he sees the average man recognises himself in the hero, and vociferates his approbation.

The sensibility that came into vogue during the eighteenth century was of a finer grain than its modern counterpart. It studied delicacy, and sought a cultivated enjoyment in evanescent shades of feeling, and the fantasies of unsubstantial grief. The real Princess of Hans Andersen's story, who passed a miserable night because there was a small bean concealed beneath the twenty eider-down beds on which she slept, might stand for a type of the aristocracy of feeling that took a pride in these ridiculous susceptibilities. The modern sentimentalist works in a coarser material. That ancient, subtle, and treacherous affinity among the emotions, whereby religious exaltation has before now been made the ally of the unpurified passions, is parodied by him in a simpler and more useful device. By alleging a moral purpose he is enabled to gratify the prurience of his public and to raise p. 83 them in their own muddy conceit at one and the same time. The plea serves well with those artless readers who have been accustomed to consider the moral of a story as something separable from imagination, expression, and style—a quality, it may be, inherent in the plot, or a kind of appendix, exercising a retrospective power of jurisdiction and absolution over the extravagances of the piece to which it is affixed. Let virtue be rewarded, and they are content though it should never be vitally imagined or portrayed. If their eyes were opened they might cry with Brutus—"O miserable Virtue! Thou art but a phrase, and I have followed thee as though thou wert a reality."

It is in quite another kind, however, that the modern purveyor of sentiment exercises his most characteristic talent. There are certain real and deeply-rooted feelings, common to humanity, concerning which, in their normal operation, a grave reticence is natural. They are universal in their appeal, men would be ashamed not to feel them, and it is no small part of the business of life to keep them under strict control. Here is the sentimental p. 84 hucksters most valued opportunity. He tears these primary instincts from the wholesome privacy that shelters them in life, and cries them up from his booth in the market-place. The elemental forces of human life, which beget shyness in children, and touch the spirits of the wise to solemn acquiescence, awaken him to noisier declamation. He patronises the stern laws of love and pity, hawking them like indulgences, cheapening and commanding them like the medicines of a mountebank. The censure of his critics he impudently meets by pointing to his wares: are not some of the most sacred properties of humanity—sympathy with suffering, family affection, filial devotion, and the rest—displayed upon his stall? Not thus shall he evade the charges brought against him. It is the sensual side of the tender emotions that he exploits for the comfort of the million. All the intricacies which life offers to the will and the intellect he lards and obliterates by the timely effusion of tearful sentiment. His humanitarianism is a more popular, as it is an easier, ideal than humanity—it asks no expense p. 85 of thought. There is a scanty public in England for tragedy or for comedy: the characters and situations handled by the sentimentalist might perchance furnish comedy with a theme; but he stilts them for a tragic performance, and they tumble into watery bathos, where a numerous public awaits them.

A similar degradation of the intellectual elements that are present in all good literature is practised by those whose single aim is to provoke laughter. In much of our so-called comic writing a superabundance of boisterous animal spirits, restrained from more practical expression by the ordinances of civil society, finds outlet and relief.

The grimaces and caperings of buffoonery, the gymnastics of the punster and the parodist, the revels of pure nonsense may be, at their best, a refreshment and delight, but they are not comedy, and have proved in effect not a little hostile to the existence of comedy. The prevalence of jokers, moreover, spoils the game of humour; the sputter and sparkle of their made jokes interferes with that luminous contemplation of the incongruities p. 86of life and the universe which is humour's essence. All that is ludicrous depends on some disproportion: Comedy judges the actual world by contrasting it with an ideal of sound sense, Humour reveals it in its true dimensions by turning on it the light of imagination and poetry. The perception of these incongruities, which are eternal, demands some expense of intellect; a cheaper amusement may be enjoyed by him who is content to take his stand on his own habits and prejudices and to laugh at all that does not square with them. This was the method of the age which, in the abysmal profound of waggery, engendered that portentous birth, the comic paper. Foreigners, it is said, do not laugh at the wit of these journals, and no wonder, for only a minute study of the customs and preoccupations of certain sections of English society could enable them to understand the point of view. From time to time one or another of the writers who are called upon for their weekly tale of jokes seems struggling upward to the free domain of Comedy; but in vain, his public holds him down, and compels him to laugh p. 87in chains. Some day, perchance, a literary historian, filled with the spirit of Cervantes or of Molière, will give account of the Victorian era, and, not disdaining small things, will draw a picture of the society which inspired and controlled so resolute a jocularity. Then, at last, will the spirit of Comedy recognise that these were indeed what they claimed to be—comic papers.

"The style is the man;" but the social and rhetorical influences adulterate and debase it, until not one man in a thousand achieves his birthright, or claims his second self. The fire of the soul burns all too feebly, and warms itself by the reflected heat from the society around it. We give back words of tepid greeting, without improvement. We talk to our fellows in the phrases we learn from them, which come to mean less and less as they grow worn with use. Then we exaggerate and distort, heaping epithet upon epithet in the endeavour to get a little warmth out of the smouldering pile. The quiet cynicism of our everyday demeanour is open and shameless, we callously anticipate objections founded on the p. 88well-known vacuity of our seeming emotions, and assure our friends that we are "truly" grieved or "sincerely" rejoiced at their hap—as if joy or grief that really exists were some rare and precious brand of joy or grief. In its trivial conversational uses so simple and pure a thing as joy becomes a sandwich-man—humanity degraded to an advertisement. The poor dejected word shuffles along through the mud in the service of the sleek trader who employs it, and not until it meets with a poet is it rehabilitated and restored to dignity.

This is no indictment of society, which came into being before literature, and, in all the distraction of its multifarious concerns, can hardly keep a school for Style. It is rather a demonstration of the necessity, amid the wealthy disorder of modern civilisation, for poetic diction. One of the hardest of a poet's tasks is the search for his vocabulary. Perhaps in some idyllic pasture-land of Utopia there may have flourished a state where division of labour was unknown, where community of ideas, as well as of property, was absolute, and where the language of every day ran p. 89clear into poetry without the need of a refining process. They say that Cædmon was a cow-keeper: but the shepherds of Theocritus and Virgil are figments of a courtly brain, and Wordsworth himself, in his boldest flights of theory, was forced to allow of selection. Even by selection from among the chaos of implements that are in daily use around him, a poet can barely equip himself with a choice of words sufficient for his needs; he must have recourse to his predecessors; and so it comes about that the poetry of the modern world is a store-house of obsolete diction. The most surprising characteristic of the right poetic diction, whether it draw its vocabulary from near at hand, or avail itself of the far-fetched inheritance preserved by the poets, is its matchless sincerity. Something of extravagance there may be in those brilliant clusters of romantic words that are everywhere found in the work of Shakespeare, or Spenser, or Keats, but they are the natural leafage and fruitage of a luxuriant imagination, which, lacking these, could not attain to its full height. Only by the p. 90energy of the arts can a voice be given to the subtleties and raptures of emotional experience; ordinary social intercourse affords neither opportunity nor means for this fervour of self-revelation. And if the highest reach of poetry is often to be found in the use of common colloquialisms, charged with the intensity of restrained passion, this is not due to a greater sincerity of expression, but to the strength derived from dramatic situation. Where speech spends itself on its subject, drama stands idle; but where the dramatic stress is at its greatest, three or four words may enshrine all the passion of the moment. Romeo's apostrophe from under the balcony—

O, speak again, bright Angel! for thou art
As glorious to this night, being o'er my head,
As is a winged messenger of heaven
Unto the white-upturned wond'ring eyes
Of mortals that fall back to gaze on him,
When he bestrides the lazy-pacing clouds,
And sails upon the bosom of the air—

though it breathe the soul of romance, must yield, for sheer effect, to his later soliloquy, spoken when the news of Juliet's death is brought to him,

p. 91Well, Juliet, I will lie with thee to-night.

And even the constellated glories of *Paradise Lost* are less moving than the plain words wherein Samson forecasts his approaching end—

So much I feel my genial spirits droop,
My hopes all flat; Nature within me seems
In all her functions weary of herself;
My race of glory run and race of shame,
And I shall shortly be with them that rest.

Here are simple words raised to a higher power and animated with a purer intention than they carry in ordinary life. It is this unfailing note of sincerity, eloquent or laconic, that has made poetry the teacher of prose. Phrases which, to all seeming, might have been hit on by the first comer, are often cut away from their poetical context and robbed of their musical value that they may be transferred to the service of prose. They bring with them, down to the valley, a wafted sense of some region of higher thought and purer feeling. They bear, perhaps, no marks of curious diction to know them by. Whence comes the irresistible pathos of the lines—

p. 92I cannot but remember such things were
That were most precious to me?

The thought, the diction, the syntax, might all occur in prose. Yet when once the stamp of poetry has been put upon a cry that is as old as humanity, prose desists from rivalry, and is content to quote. Some of the greatest prose-writers have not disdained the help of these borrowed graces for the crown of their fabric. In this way De Quincey widens the imaginative range of his prose, and sets back the limits assigned to prose diction. So too, Charles Lamb, interweaving the stuff of experience with phrases quoted or altered from the poets, illuminates both life and poetry, letting his sympathetic humour play now on the warp of the texture, and now on the woof. The style of Burke furnishes a still better example, for the spontaneous evolution of his prose might be thought to forbid the inclusion of borrowed fragments. Yet whenever he is deeply stirred, memories of Virgil, Milton, or the English Bible rise to his aid, almost as if strong emotion could express itself in no other p. 93language. Even the poor invectives of political controversy gain a measure of dignity from the skilful application of some famous line; the touch of the poet's sincerity rests on them for a moment, and seems to lend them an alien splendour. It is like the blessing of a priest, invoked by the pious, or by the worldly, for the good success of whatever business they have in hand. Poetry has no temporal ends to serve, no livelihood to earn, and is under no temptation to cog and lie: wherefore prose pays respect to that loftier calling, and that more unblemished sincerity.

Insincerity, on the other hand, is the commonest vice of style. It is not to be avoided, except in the rarest cases, by those to whom the written use of language is unfamiliar;

so that a shepherd who talks pithy, terse sense will be unable to express himself in a letter without having recourse to the *Ready Letter-writer*—"This comes hoping to find you well, as it also leaves me at present"—and a soldier, without the excuse of ignorance, will describe a successful advance as having been made against "a thick hail of bullets." It permeates_{p. 94} ordinary journalism, and all writing produced under commercial pressure. It taints the work of the young artist, caught by the romantic fever, who glories in the wealth of vocabulary discovered to him by the poets, and seeks often in vain for a thought stalwart enough to wear that glistering armour. Hence it is that the masters of style have always had to preach restraint, self-denial, austerity. His style is a man's own; yet how hard it is to come by! It is a man's bride, to be won by labours and agonies that bespeak a heroic lover. If he prove unable to endure the trial, there are cheaper beauties, nearer home, easy to be conquered, and faithless to their conqueror. Taking up with them, he may attain a brief satisfaction, but he will never redeem his quest.

As a body of practical rules, the negative precepts of asceticism bring with them a certain chill. The page is dull; it is so easy to lighten it with some flash of witty irrelevance: the argument is long and tedious, why not relieve it by wandering into some of those green enclosures that open alluring doors upon the wayside? To roam p. 95 at will, spring-heeled, high-hearted, and catching at all good fortunes, is the ambition of the youth, ere yet he has subdued himself to a destination. The principle of self-denial seems at first sight a treason done to genius, which was always privileged to be wilful. In this view literature is a fortuitous series of happy thoughts and heaven-sent findings. But the end of that plan is beggary. Sprightly talk about the first object that meets the eye and the indulgence of vagabond habits soon degenerate to a professional garrulity, a forced face of dismal cheer, and a settled dislike of strenuous exercise. The economies and abstinences of discipline promise a kinder fate than this. They test and strengthen purpose, without which no great work comes into being. They save the expenditure of energy on those pastimes and diversions which lead no nearer to the goal. To reject the images and arguments that proffer a casual assistance yet are not to be brought under the perfect control of the main theme is difficult; how should it be otherwise, for if they were not already dear to the writer they would not have volunteered their aid.

p. 96 It is the more difficult, in that to refuse the unfit is no warrant of better help to come. But to accept them is to fall back for good upon a makeshift, and to hazard the enterprise in a hubbub of disorderly claims. No train of thought is strengthened by the addition of those arguments that, like camp-followers, swell the number and the noise, without bearing a part in the organisation. The danger that comes in with the employment of figures of speech, similes, and comparisons is greater still. The clearest of them may be attended by some element of grotesque or paltry association, so that while they illumine the subject they cannot truly be said to illustrate it. The noblest, including those time-honoured metaphors that draw their patent of nobility from war, love, religion, or the chase, in proportion as they are strong and of a vivid presence, are also domineering—apt to assume command of the theme long after their proper work is done. So great is the headstrong power of the finest metaphors, that an author may be incommoded by one that does his business for him handsomely, as a _{p. 97}king may suffer the oppression of a powerful ally. When a lyric begins with the splendid lines,

Love   still   has   something   of   the   sea
From whence his mother rose,

the further development of that song is already fixed and its knell rung—to the last line there is no escaping from the dazzling influences that presided over the first. Yet to carry out such a figure in detail, as Sir Charles Sedley set himself to do, tarnishes the sudden glory of the opening. The lady whom Burns called Clarinda put herself in a like quandary by beginning a song with this stanza—

Talk   not   of   Love,   it   gives   me   pain,
    For   Love   has   been   my   foe;
He   bound   me   in   an   iron   chain,
    And plunged me deep in woe.

The last two lines deserve praise—even the praise they obtained from a great lyric poet. But how is the song to be continued? Genius might answer the question; to Clarinda there came only the notion of a valuable contrast to be established between love and friendship, and a tribute to be paid to the kindly offices of the latter. The _{p. 98}verses wherein she gave effect to this idea make a poor sequel; friendship, when it is personified and set beside the tyrant god, wears very much the air of a benevolent county magistrate, whose chief duty is to keep the peace.

Figures of this sort are in no sense removable decorations, they are at one with the substance of the thought to be expressed, and are entitled to the large control they claim. Imagination, working at white heat, can fairly subdue the matter of the poem to them, or fuse them with others of the like temper, striking unity out of the composite mass. One thing only is forbidden, to treat these substantial and living metaphors as if they were elegant curiosities, ornamental excrescences, to be passed over abruptly on the way to more exacting topics. The mystics, and the mystical poets, knew better than to countenance this frivolity. Recognising that there is a profound and intimate correspondence between all physical manifestations and the life of the soul, they flung the reins on the neck of metaphor in the hope that it might carry them over that mysterious frontier. Their _{p. 99}failures and misadventures, familiarly despised as "conceits," left them floundering in absurdity. Yet not since the time of Donne and Crashaw has the full power and significance of figurative language been realised in English poetry. These poets, like some of their late descendants, were tortured by a sense of hidden meaning, and were often content with analogies that admit of no rigorous explanation. They were convinced that all intellectual truth is a parable, though its inner meaning be dark or dubious. The philosophy of friendship deals with those mathematical and physical conceptions of distance, likeness, and attraction—what if the law of bodies govern souls also, and the geometer's compasses measure more than it has entered into his heart to conceive? Is the moon a name only for a certain tonnage of dead matter, and is the law of passion parochial while the law of gravitation is universal? Mysticism will observe no such partial boundaries.

> O more than Moon!
> Draw not up seas to drown me in thy sphere,
> Weep me not dead in thine arms, but forbear
> To teach the sea what it may do too soon.

p. 100The secret of these sublime intuitions, undivined by many of the greatest poets, has been left to the keeping of transcendental religion and the Catholic Church.

Figure and ornament, therefore, are not interchangeable terms; the loftiest figurative style most conforms to the precepts of gravity and chastity. None the less there is a decorative use of figure, whereby a theme is enriched with imaginations and memories that are foreign to the main purpose. Under this head may be classed most of those allusions to the world's literature, especially to classical and Scriptural lore, which have played so considerable, yet on the whole so idle, a part in modern poetry. It is here that an inordinate love of decoration finds its opportunity and its snare. To keep the most elaborate comparison in harmony with its occasion, so that when it is completed it shall fall back easily into the emotional key of the narrative, has been the study of the great epic poets. Milton's description of the rebel legions adrift on the flaming sea p. 101is a fine instance of the difficulty felt and conquered:

> Angel forms, who lay entranced
> Thick as autumnal leaves that strow the brooks
> In Vallombrosa, where the Etrurian shades
> High over-arched embower; or scattered sedge
> Afloat, when with fierce winds Orion armed
> Hath vexed the Red-Sea coast, whose waves o'erthrew
> Busiris and his Memphian chivalry,
> While with perfidious hatred they pursued
> The sojourners of Goshen, who beheld
> From the safe shore their floating carcases
> And broken chariot-wheels. So thick bestrown,
> Abject and lost, lay these, covering the flood,
> Under amazement of their hideous change.

The comparison seems to wander away at random, obedient to the slightest touch of association. Yet in the end it is brought back, its majesty heightened, and a closer element of likeness introduced by the skilful turn that substitutes the image of the shattered Egyptian army for the former images of dead leaves and sea-weed. The incidental pictures, of the roof of shades, of the watchers from the shore, and the very name "Red Sea," fortuitous as they may seem, all lend help to the imagination in bodying forth p. 102the scene described. An earlier figure in the same book of *Paradise Lost*, because it exhibits a less conspicuous technical cunning, may even better show a poet's care for unity of tone and impression. Where Satan's prostrate bulk is compared to

> that   sea-beast
> Leviathan,   which   God   of   all   his   works
> Created hugest that swim the ocean-stream,

the picture that follows of the Norse-pilot mooring his boat under the lee of the monster is completed in a line that attunes the mind once more to all the pathos and gloom of those infernal deeps:

> while   night
> Invests the sea, and wishèd morn delays.

So masterly a handling of the figures which usage and taste prescribe to learned writers is rare indeed. The ordinary small scholar disposes of his baggage less happily. Having heaped up knowledge as a successful tradesman heaps up money, he is apt to believe that his wealth makes him free of the company of letters, and a fellow craftsman of the poets. The mark of his style p. 103is an excessive and pretentious allusiveness. It was he whom the satirist designed in that taunt, *Scire tuum nihil est nisi te scire hoc sciat alter*—"My knowledge of thy knowledge is the knowledge thou covetest." His allusions and learned periphrases elucidate nothing; they put an idle labour on the reader who understands them, and extort from baffled ignorance, at which, perhaps, they are more especially aimed, a foolish admiration. These tricks and vanities, the very corruption of ornament, will always be found while the power to acquire knowledge is more general than the strength to carry it or the skill to wield it. The collector has his proper work to do in the commonwealth of learning, but the ownership of a museum is a poor qualification for the name of artist. Knowledge has two good uses; it may be frankly communicated for the benefit of others, or it may minister matter to thought; an allusive writer often robs it of both these functions. He must needs display his possessions and his modesty at one and the same time, producing his treasures unasked, and huddling them in uncouth p. 104fashion past the gaze of the spectator, because, forsooth, he would not seem to make a rarity of them. The subject to be treated, the groundwork to be adorned, becomes the barest excuse for a profitless haphazard ostentation. This fault is very incident to the scholarly style, which often sacrifices emphasis and conviction to a futile air of encyclopædic grandeur.

Those who are repelled by this redundance of ornament, from which even great writers are not wholly exempt, have sometimes been driven by the force of reaction into a singular fallacy. The futility of these literary quirks and graces has induced them to lay art under the same interdict with ornament. Style and stylists, one will say, have no attraction for him, he had rather hear honest men utter their thoughts directly, clearly, and simply. The choice of words, says another, and the conscious manipulation of sentences, is literary foppery; the word that first offers is commonly the best, and the order in which the thoughts occur is the order to be followed. Be natural, be straightforward, they urge, and what p. 105you have to say will say itself in the best possible manner. It is a welcome lesson, no doubt, that these deluded Arcadians teach. A simple and direct style—who would not give his all to purchase that! But is it in truth so easy to be compassed? The greatest writers, when they are at the top of happy hours, attain to it, now and again. Is all this tangled contrariety of things a kind of fairyland, and does the writer, alone among men, find that a beaten foot-path opens out before him as he goes, to lead him, straight through the maze, to the goal of his desires? To think so is to build a childish dream out of facts imperfectly observed, and worthy of a closer observation. Sometimes the cry for simplicity is the reverse of what it seems, and is uttered by those who had rather hear words used in their habitual vague acceptations than submit to the cutting directness of a good writer. Habit makes obscurity grateful, and the simple style, in this view, is the style that allows thought to run automatically into its old grooves and burrows. The original writers who have combined real p. 106literary power with the heresy of ease and nature are of another kind. A brutal personality, excellently muscular, snatching at words as the handiest weapons wherewith to inflict itself, and the whole body of its thoughts and preferences, on suffering humanity, is likely enough to deride the daintiness of conscious art. Such a writer is William Cobbett, who has often been praised for the manly simplicity of his style, which he raised into a kind of creed. His power is undeniable; his diction, though he knew it not, both choice and chaste; yet page after page of his writing suggests only the reflection that here is a prodigal waste of good English. He bludgeons all he touches, and spends the same monotonous emphasis on his dislike of tea and on his hatred of the Government. His is the simplicity of a crude and violent mind, concerned only with giving forcible expression to its unquestioned prejudices. Irrelevance, the besetting sin of the ill-educated, he glories in, so that his very weakness puts on the semblance of strength, and helps to wield the hammer.

p. 107It is not to be denied that there is a native force of temperament which can make itself felt even through illiterate carelessness. "Literary gentlemen, editors, and critics," says Thoreau, himself by no means a careless writer, "think that they know how to write, because they have studied grammar and rhetoric; but they are egregiously mistaken. The *art* of composition is as simple as the discharge of a bullet from a rifle, and its masterpieces imply an infinitely greater force behind them." This true saying introduces us to the hardest problem of criticism, the paradox of literature, the stumbling-block of rhetoricians. To analyse the precise method whereby a great personality can make itself felt in words, even while it neglects and contemns the study of words, would be to lay bare the secrets of religion and life—it is beyond human competence. Nevertheless a brief and diffident consideration of the matter may bring thus much comfort, that the seeming contradiction is no discredit cast on letters, but takes its origin rather from too narrow and pedantic a view of the scope of letters.

p. 108Words are things: it is useless to try to set them in a world apart. They exist in books only by accident, and for one written there are a thousand, infinitely more powerful, spoken. They are deeds: the man who brings word of a lost battle can work no comparable effect with the muscles of his arm; Iago's breath is as truly laden with poison and murder as the fangs of the cobra and the drugs of the assassin. Hence the sternest education in the use of words is least of all to be gained in the schools, which cultivate verbiage in a highly artificial state of seclusion. A soldier cares little for poetry, because it is the exercise of power that he loves, and he is accustomed to do more with his words than give pleasure. To keep language in immediate touch with reality, to lade it with action and passion, to utter it hot from the heart of determination, is to exhibit it in the plenitude of power. All this may be achieved without the smallest study of literary models, and is consistent with a perfect neglect of literary canons. It is not the logical content of the word, but the whole mesh of its conditions, p. 109including the character, circumstances, and attitude of the speaker, that is its true strength. "Damn" is often the feeblest of expletives, and "as you please" may be the dirge of an empire. Hence it is useless to look to the grammarian, or the critic, for a lesson in strength of style; the laws that he has framed, good enough in themselves, are current only in his own abstract world. A breath of hesitancy will sometimes make trash of a powerful piece of eloquence; and even in writing, a thing three times said, and each time said badly, may be of more effect than that terse, full, and final expression which the doctors rightly commend. The art of language, regarded as a question of pattern and cadence, or even as a question of logic and thought-sequence, is a highly abstract study; for although, as has been said, you can do almost anything with words, with words alone you can do next to nothing. The realm where speech holds sway is a narrow shoal or reef, shaken, contorted, and upheaved by volcanic action, beaten upon, bounded, and invaded by the ocean of silence: whoso would be lord of p. 110the earth must first tame the fire and the sea. Dramatic and narrative writing are happy in this, that action and silence are a part of their material; the story-teller or the playwright can make of words a background and definition for deeds, a framework for those silences that are more telling than any speech. Here lies an escape from the poverty of content and method to which self-portraiture and self-expression are liable; and therefore are epic and drama rated above all other kinds of poetry. The greater force of the objective treatment is witnessed by many essayists and lyrical poets, whose ambition has led them, sooner or later, to attempt the novel or the play. There are weaknesses inherent in all direct self-revelation; the thing, perhaps, is greatly said, yet there is no great occasion for the saying of it; a fine reticence is observed, but it is, after all, an easy reticence, with none of the dramatic splendours of reticence on the rack. In the midst of his pleasant confidences the essayist is brought up short by the question, "Why must you still be talking?" Even the passionate lyric feels the need of external p. 111 authorisation, and some of the finest of lyrical poems, like the Willow Song of Desdemona, or Wordsworth's *Solitary Reaper*, are cast in a dramatic mould, that beauty of diction may be vitalised by an imagined situation. More than others the dramatic art is an enemy to the desultory and the superfluous, sooner than others it will cast away all formal grace of expression that it may come home more directly to the business and bosoms of men. Its great power and scope are shown well in this, that it can find high uses for the commonest stuff of daily speech and the emptiest phrases of daily intercourse.

Simplicity and strength, then, the vigorous realistic quality of impromptu utterance, and an immediate relation with the elementary facts of life, are literary excellences best known in the drama, and in its modern fellow and rival, the novel. The dramatist and novelist create their own characters, set their own scenes, lay their own plots, and when all has been thus prepared, the right word is born in the purple, an inheritor of great opportunities, all its virtues magnified by p. 112 the glamour of its high estate. Writers on philosophy, morals, or æsthetics, critics, essayists, and dealers in soliloquy generally, cannot hope, with their slighter means, to attain to comparable effects. They work at two removes from life; the terms that they handle are surrounded by the vapours of discussion, and are rewarded by no instinctive response. Simplicity, in its most regarded sense, is often beyond their reach; the matter of their discourse is intricate, and the most they can do is to employ patience, care, and economy of labour; the meaning of their words is not obvious, and they must go aside to define it. The strength of their writing has limits set for it by the nature of the chosen task, and any transgression of these limits is punished by a fall into sheer violence. All writing partakes of the quality of the drama, there is always a situation involved, the relation, namely, between the speaker and the hearer. A gentleman in black, expounding his views, or narrating his autobiography to the first comer, can expect no such warmth of response as greets the dying speech of the baffled patriot; yet he p. 113 too may take account of the reasons that prompt speech, may display sympathy and tact, and avoid the faults of senility. The only character that can lend strength to his words is his own, and he sketches it while he states his opinions; the only attitude that can ennoble his sayings is implied in the very arguments he uses. Who does not know the curious blank effect of eloquence overstrained or out of place? The phrasing may be exquisite, the thought well-knit, the emotion genuine, yet all is, as it were, dumb-show where no community of feeling exists between the speaker and his audience. A similar false note is struck by any speaker or writer who misapprehends his position or forgets his disqualifications, by newspaper writers using language that is seemly only in one who stakes his life on his words, by preachers exceeding the license of fallibility, by moralists condemning frailty, by speculative traders deprecating frank ways of hazard, by Satan rebuking sin.

"How many things are there," exclaims the wise Verulam, "which a man cannot, with any face or comeliness, say or do himself! A man's p. 114person hath many proper relations which he cannot put off. A man cannot speak to his son but as a father; to his wife, but as a husband; to his enemy but upon terms; whereas a friend may speak as the case requires, and not as it sorteth with the person." The like "proper relations" govern writers, even where their audience is unknown to them. It has often been remarked how few are the story-tellers who can introduce themselves, so much as by a passing reflection or sentiment, without a discordant effect. The friend who saves the situation is found in one and another of the creatures of their art.

For those who must play their own part the effort to conceal themselves is of no avail. The implicit attitude of a writer makes itself felt; an undue swelling of his subject to heroic dimensions, an unwarrantable assumption of sympathy, a tendency to truck with friends or with enemies by the way, are all possible indications of weakness, which move even the least skilled of readers to discount what is said, as they catch here and there a glimpse of the old pot-companion, or the young p. 115dandy, behind the imposing literary mask. Strong writers are those who, with every reserve of power, seek no exhibition of strength. It is as if language could not come by its full meaning save on the lips of those who regard it as an evil necessity. Every word is torn from them, as from a reluctant witness. They come to speech as to a last resort, when all other ways have failed. The bane of a literary education is that it induces talkativeness, and an overweening confidence in words. But those whose words are stark and terrible seem almost to despise words.

With words literature begins, and to words it must return. Coloured by the neighbourhood of silence, solemnised by thought or steeled by action, words are still its only means of rising above words. "*Accedat verbum ad elementum*," said St. Ambrose, "*et fiat sacramentum.*" So the elementary passions, pity and love, wrath and terror, are not in themselves poetical; they must be wrought upon by the word to become poetry. In no other way can suffering be transformed to pathos, or horror reach its apotheosis in tragedy.

p. 116When all has been said, there remains a residue capable of no formal explanation. Language, this array of conventional symbols loosely strung together, and blown about by every wandering breath, is miraculously vital and expressive, justifying not a few of the myriad superstitions that have always attached to its use. The same words are free to all, yet no wealth or distinction of vocabulary is needed for a group of words to take the stamp of an individual mind and character. "As a quality of style" says Mr. Pater, "soul is a fact." To resolve how words, like bodies, become transparent when they are inhabited by that luminous reality, is a higher pitch than metaphysic wit can fly. Ardent persuasion and deep feeling enkindle words, so that the weakest take on glory. The humblest and most despised of common phrases may be the chosen vessel for the next avatar of the spirit. It is the old problem, to be met only by the old solution of the Platonist, that

Soul is form, and doth the body make.

The soul is able to inform language by some p. 117strange means other than the choice and arrangement of words and phrases. Real novelty of vocabulary is impossible; in the matter of language we lead a parasitical existence, and are always quoting. Quotations, conscious or unconscious, vary in kind according as the mind is active to work upon them and make them its own. In its grossest and most servile form quotation is a lazy folly; a thought has received some signal or notorious expression, and as often as the old sense, or something like it, recurs, the old phrase rises to the lips. This degenerates to simple phrase-mongering, and those who practise it are not vigilantly jealous of their meaning. Such an expression as "fine by degrees and beautifully less" is often no more than a bloated equivalent for a single word—say "diminishing" or "shrinking." Quotations like this are the warts and excremental parts of language; the borrowings of good writers are never thus superfluous, their quotations are appropriations. Whether it be by some witty turn given to a well-known line, by an original setting for an old saw, or by a new and p. 118unlooked-for analogy, the stamp of the borrower is put upon the goods he borrows, and he becomes part owner. Plagiarism is a crime only where writing is a trade; expression need never be bound by the law of copyright while it follows thought, for thought, as some great thinker has observed, is free. The words were once Shakespeare's; if only you can feel them as he did, they are yours now no less than his. The best quotations, the best translations, the best thefts, are all equally new and original works. From quotation, at least, there is no escape, inasmuch as we learn language from others. All common phrases that do the dirty work of the world are quotations—poor things, and not our own. Who first said that a book would "repay perusal," or that any gay scene was "bright with all the colours of the rainbow"? There is no need to condemn these phrases, for language has a vast deal of inferior work to do. The expression of thought, temperament, attitude, is not the whole of its business. It is only a literary fop or doctrinaire who will attempt to remint all the small defaced coinage p. 119that passes through his hands, only a lisping young fantastico who will refuse all conventional garments and all conventional speech. At a modern wedding the frock-coat is worn, the presents are "numerous and costly," and there is an "ovation accorded to the happy pair." These things are part of our public civilisation, a decorous and accessible uniform, not to be lightly set aside. But let it be a friend of your own who is to marry, a friend of your own who dies, and you are to express yourself—the problem is changed, you feel all the difficulties of the art of style, and fathom something of the depth of your unskill. Forbidden silence, we should be in a poor way indeed.

Single words too we plagiarise when we use them without realisation and mastery of their meaning. The best argument for a succinct style is this, that if you use words you do not need, or do not understand, you cannot use them well. It is not what a word means, but what it means to you, that is of the deepest import. Let it be a weak word, with a poor history behind it, if you p. 120 have done good thinking with it, you may yet use it to surprising advantage. But if, on the other hand, it be a strong word that has never aroused more than a misty idea and a flickering emotion in your mind, here lies your danger. You may use it, for there is none to hinder; and it will betray you. The commonest Saxon words prove explosive machines in the hands of rash impotence. It is perhaps a certain uneasy consciousness of danger, a suspicion that weakness of soul cannot wield these strong words, that makes debility avoid them, committing itself rather, as if by some pre-established affinity, to the vaguer Latinised vocabulary. Yet they are not all to be avoided, and their quality in practice will depend on some occult ability in their employer. For every living person, if the material were obtainable, a separate historical dictionary might be compiled, recording where each word was first heard or seen, where and how it was first used. The references are utterly beyond recovery; but such a register would throw a strange light on individual styles. The eloquent trifler, whose stock of words p. 121 has been accumulated by a pair of light fingers, would stand denuded of his plausible pretences as soon as it were seen how roguishly he came by his eloquence. There may be literary quality, it is well to remember, in the words of a parrot, if only its cage has been happily placed; meaning and soul there cannot be. Yet the voice will sometimes be mistaken, by the carelessness of chance listeners, for a genuine utterance of humanity; and the like is true in literature. But writing cannot be luminous and great save in the hands of those whose words are their own by the indefeasible title of conquest. Life is spent in learning the meaning of great words, so that some idle proverb, known for years and accepted perhaps as a truism, comes home, on a day, like a blow. "If there were not a God," said Voltaire, "it would be necessary to invent him." Voltaire had therefore a right to use the word, but some of those who use it most, if they would be perfectly sincere, should enclose it in quotation marks. Whole nations go for centuries without coining names for certain virtues; is it credible p. 122 that among other peoples, where the names exists the need for them is epidemic? The author of the *Ecclesiastial Polity* puts a bolder and truer face on the matter. "Concerning that Faith, Hope, and Charity," he writes, "without which there can be no salvation, was there ever any mention made saving only in that Law which God himself hath from Heaven revealed? There is not in the world a syllable muttered with certain truth concerning any of these three, more than hath been supernaturally received from the mouth of the eternal God." Howsoever they came to us, we have the words; they, and many other terms of tremendous import, are bandied about from mouth to mouth and alternately enriched or impoverished in meaning. Is the "Charity" of St. Paul's Epistle one with the charity of "charity-blankets"? Are the "crusades" of Godfrey and of the great St. Louis, where knightly achievement did homage to the religious temper, essentially the same as that process of harrying the wretched and the outcast for which the muddle-headed, greasy citizen of p. 123 to-day invokes the same high name? Of a truth, some kingly words fall to a lower estate than Nebuchadnezzar.

Here, among words, our lot is cast, to make or mar. It is in this obscure thicket, overgrown with weeds, set with thorns, and haunted by shadows, this World of Words, as the Elizabethans finely called it, that we wander, eternal pioneers, during the course of our mortal lives. To be overtaken by a master, one who comes along with the gaiety of assured skill and courage, with the gravity of unflinching purpose, to make the crooked ways straight and the rough places plain, is to gain fresh confidence from despair. He twines wreaths of the entangling ivy, and builds ramparts of the thorns. He blazes his mark upon the secular oaks, as a guidance to later travellers, and coaxes flame from heaps of mouldering rubbish. There is no sense of cheer like this. Sincerity, clarity, candour, power, seem real once more, real and easy. In the light of great literary achievement, straight and wonderful, like the roads of the ancient Romans, barbarism torments p. 124 the mind like a riddle. Yet there are the dusky barbarians!—fleeing from the harmonious tread of the ordered legions, running to hide themselves in the morass of vulgar sentiment, to ambush their nakedness in the sand-pits of low thought.

It is a venerable custom to knit up the speculative consideration of any subject with the counsels of practical wisdom. The words of this essay have been vain indeed if the idea that style may be imparted by tuition has eluded them, and survived. There is a useful art of Grammar, which takes for its province the right and the wrong in speech. Style deals only with what is permissible to all, and even revokes, on occasion, the rigid laws of Grammar or countenances offences against them. Yet no one is a better judge of equity for ignorance of the law, and grammatical practice offers a fair field wherein to acquire ease, accuracy and versatility. The formation of sentences, the sequence of verbs, the marshalling of the ranks of auxiliaries are all, in a sense, to be learned. There p. 125 is a kind of inarticulate disorder to which writers are liable, quite distinct from a bad style, and caused chiefly by lack of exercise. An unpractised writer will sometimes send a beautiful and powerful phrase jostling along in the midst of a clumsy sentence—like a crowned king escorted by a mob.

But Style cannot be taught. Imitation of the masters, or of some one chosen master, and the constant purging of language by a severe criticism, have their uses, not to be belittled; they have also their dangers. The greater part of what is called the teaching of style must always be negative, bad habits may be broken down, old malpractices prohibited. The pillory and the stocks are hardly educational agents, but they make it easier for honest men to enjoy their own. If style could really be taught, it is a question whether its teachers should not be regarded as mischief-makers and enemies of mankind. The Rosicrucians professed to have found the philosopher's stone, and the shadowy sages of modern Thibet are said, by those who speak for them, to have compassed the p. 126instantaneous transference of bodies from place to place. In either case, the holders of these secrets have laudably refused to publish them, lest avarice and malice should run amuck in human society. A similar fear might well visit the conscience of one who should dream that he had divulged to the world at large what can be done with language. Of this there is no danger; rhetoric, it is true, does put fluency, emphasis, and other warlike equipments at the disposal of evil forces, but style, like the Christian religion, is one of those open secrets which are most easily and most effectively kept by the initiate from age to age. Divination is the only means of access to these mysteries. The formal attempt to impart a good style is like the melancholy task of the teacher of gesture and oratory; some palpable faults are soon corrected; and, for the rest, a few conspicuous mannerisms, a few theatrical postures, not truly expressive, and a high tragical strut, are all that can be imparted. The truth of the old Roman teachers of rhetoric is here witnessed afresh, to be a good orator it is first of all necessary to be a good man. Good p. 127style is the greatest of revealers,—it lays bare the soul. The soul of the cheat shuns nothing so much. "Always be ready to speak your minds" said Blake, "and a base man will avoid you." But to insist that he also shall speak his mind is to go a step further, it is to take from the impostor his wooden leg, to prohibit his lucrative whine, his mumping and his canting, to force the poor silly soul to stand erect among its fellows and declare itself. His occupation is gone, and he does not love the censor who deprives him of the weapons of his mendicity.

All style is gesture, the gesture of the mind and of the soul. Mind we have in common, inasmuch as the laws of right reason are not different for different minds. Therefore clearness and arrangement can be taught, sheer incompetence in the art of expression can be partly remedied. But who shall impose laws upon the soul? It is thus of common note that one may dislike or even hate a particular style while admiring its facility, its strength, its skilful adaptation to the matter set forth. Milton, a chaster and more unerring p. 128master of the art than Shakespeare, reveals no such lovable personality. While persons count for much, style, the index to persons, can never count for little. "Speak," it has been said, "that I may know you"—voice-gesture is more than feature. Write, and after you have attained to some control over the instrument, you write yourself down whether you will or no. There is no vice, however unconscious, no virtue, however shy, no touch of meanness or of generosity in your character, that will not pass on to the paper. You anticipate the Day of Judgment and furnish the recording angel with material. The Art of Criticism in literature, so often decried and given a subordinate place among the arts, is none other than the art of reading and interpreting these written evidences. Criticism has been popularly opposed to creation, perhaps because the kind of creation that it attempts is rarely achieved, and so the world forgets that the main business of Criticism, after all, is not to legislate, nor to classify, but to raise the dead. Graves, at its command, have waked their sleepers, oped, and p. 129let them forth. It is by the creative power of this art that the living man is reconstructed from the litter of blurred and fragmentary paper documents that he has left to posterity.

Milton Keynes UK
Ingram Content Group UK Ltd.
UKHW050430290324
440175UK00013B/778

EAGUE IN THE WORLD!

£5.50

THE OFFICIAL FA PREMIER LEAGUE ANNUAL 1996

Welcome to the third Official FA Premier League Annual for youngsters. This year our friends at Grandreams have provided even more pages filled with all the excitement of the best soccer league in the world – the FA Premier League.

The Diary of a Season tells the dramatic story of the 1995-96 campaign. The twenty club profiles give you tons of vital information on all the Championship contenders for the 1996-97 season – and there are some great features on the battle for promotion and the Premiership's top players.

We hope you continue to enjoy reading and collecting these FA Premier League Annuals – they help to keep football's young fans informed about our League and are therefore an important part of the soccer scene.

Enjoy your football!

RICK PARRY
Chief Executive
FA Premier League

THE F.A. PREMIER LEAGUE

© 1996 The FA Premier League

Written and compiled by Tony Lynch
Designed by Stuart Perry

All facts believed correct at the time of going to press

Published by Grandreams Ltd
Jadwin House
205-211 Kentish Town Road
London NW5 2JU

Printed in Belgium.

DON'T MISS THE **GREAT FA PREMIER LEAGUE COMPETITION** ON PAGE 61 – THERE ARE SOME GREAT PRIZES TO BE WON!

CONTENTS ....

ARSENAL

Steve Bould wins the ball against Middlesbrough

Address: Arsenal Stadium, Highbury
London N5 1BU
Telephone: 0171-226 0304
Ticket information 0171-226 0304
Fax: 0171-226 0329
Current Ground Capacity: 38,500
all-seated
Pitch Size: 110 x 73 yards
Chairman: PD Hill-Wood
Vice-Chairman: David Dein
Chief Executive/Secretary: KJ Friar
Assistant Secretary: David Miles
Commercial Manager: John Hazell
Marketing Manager: Phil Carling
Community Scheme Officer:
A Sefton
Youth Development Officer:
T Murphy
Team Manager:
Assistant Manager/Coach: Stewart Houston
Physio: Gary Lewin
Reserve Coach: George Armstrong
Youth Coach: Pat Rice
Nickname: The Gunners
Team Colours: Red shirts with white sleeve, white shorts, red/white socks

ROLL OF HONOUR

League Champions: 1930-31, 1932-33, 1933-34, 1934-35, 1937-38, 1947-48, 1952-53, 1970-71, 1988-89, 1990-91 (10 times)
FA Cup Winners: 1930, 1936, 1950, 1971, 1979, 1993 (6 times)
FA Cup & League 'Double' Achieved: 1970-71 (once)
League Cup winners: 1987, 1993 (twice)
Charity Shield Winners: 1930, 1931, 1933, 1934, 1938, 1948, 1953, 1991-shared (8 times)
European Cup-Winners' Cup Winners: 1994 (once)
UEFA Cup Winners: 1970 (once)

OTHER RECORDS

Record Attendance: 73,295 v Sunderland, First Division 9.3.1935
Record League Victory: 12-0 v Loughborough Town, Second Division 12.3.1900
Record Defeat: 0-8 v Loughborough Town, Second Division 12.12.1896
Record Cup Victory: 11-1 v Darwen, FA Cup Third Round, 9.1.1932
Most League Goals in a Season: 127 First Division 1930-31
Most Individual League Goals in a Season: 42 by Ted Drake, 1934-35
Most League Goals in Aggregate: 150 by Cliff Bastin, between 1930-1947
Most League Appearances: 558 by David O'Leary between 1975-1993
Most Capped Player: Kenny Sansom 77 times for England
Record Transfer Out: David Rocastle to Leeds United for £2 million
Record Transfer In: Dennis Bergkamp from Inter Milan for £7.5 million

PREMIERSHIP PERFORMANCE 1995-96

P	W	D	L	F	A	Pts	Pos
38	17	12	9	49	32	63	5th

Top Scorer: Ian Wright 15
Highest Attendance: 38,323 v Liverpool

ASTON VILLA

Address: Villa Park, Trinity Road, Birmingham B6 6HE
Telephone: 0121- 327 2299
Ticket information: 0891 121848
Fax: 0121-322 2107
Current Ground Capacity: 40,310
Pitch Size: 115 x 75 yards
President: HJ Musgrove
Chairman: HD Ellis
Secretary: Steven Stride
Youth Development Officer: Peter Withe
Team Manager: Brian Little
Assistant Manager: Allan Evans
Coach: John Gregory
Physio: Jim Walker
Youth Coach: Tony McAndrew
Nickname: The Villans
Team Colours: Claret shirts with light blue sleeves, white shorts, claret/blue socks

ROLL OF HONOUR

League Champions: 1893-94, 1895-96, 1896-97, 1898-99, 1899-1900, 1909-10, 1980-81 (7 times)
FA Cup Winners: 1887, 1895, 1897, 1905, 1913, 1920, 1957 (7 times)
FA Cup & League 'Double' Achieved: 1896-97 (once)
League Cup winners: 1961, 1975, 1977, 1994, 1996 (5 times)
Charity Shield Winners: 1981-shared (once)
European Cup-Winners: 1982 (once)
European Super Cup Winners: 1982 (once)

OTHER RECORDS

Record Attendance: 76,588 v Derby County, FA Cup Sixth Round 2.3.1946
Record League Victory: 12-2 v Accrington Stanley First Division 12.3.1892
Record Defeat: 1-8 v Blackburn Rovers, FA Cup Third Round 16.2.1889
Record Cup Victory: 13-0 v Wednesbury Old Athletic, FA Cup First Round 30.10.1886
Most League Goals in a Season: 128 First Division,1930-31
Most Individual League Goals in a Season: 49 by Pongo Waring in 1930-31
Most League Goals in Aggregate: 215 by Harry Hampton between 1904-1915
Most League Appearances: 561 by Charlie Aitken between 1961-1976
Most Capped Player: Paul McGrath 51 times for Republic of Ireland
Record Transfer Out: David Platt to Bari for £5.5 million
Record Transfer In: Savo Milosevic from Partisan Belgrade for £3.5 million

Villa striker Savo Milosevic

PREMIERSHIP PERFORMANCE 1995-96

P	W	D	L	F	A	Pts	Pos
38	18	9	11	52	35	63	4th

Top Scorer: Dwight Yorke 17
Highest Attendance: 39,336 V Manchester City

BLACKBURN ROVERS

Address: Ewood Park, Blackburn
BB2 4JF
Telephone: 01245 698888
Ticket information: 01245 671666
Fax: 01245 671042
Current Ground Capacity: 31,089
Pitch Size: 115 x 72 yards
Chairman: RD Coar
Vice-Chairman: RL Matthewman
Secretary: John W Howarth FAAI
Commercial Manager: Ken Beamish
Youth Development Officer:
J Furnell
Director of Football: Kenny Dalglish
MBE
Team Manager: Ray Harford
Coach: Tony Parkes
Physio: Steve Foster
Nickname: Rovers
Team Colours: Blue and white halved
shirts, white shorts, white socks

Bottom right: **Rovers' defender
Colin Hendry**

Below: **Tim Flowers gives the
orders**

ROLL OF HONOUR

League Champions: 1911-12, 1913-14, 1994-95 (3 times)
FA Cup Winners: 1884, 1885, 1886, 1890, 1891, 1928 (6 times)
Charity Shield Winners: 1912 (once)

OTHER RECORDS

Record Attendance: 61,783 v Bolton Wanderers, FA Cup Sixth Round 2.3.1929
Record League Victory: 9-0 v Middlesbrough, Second Division 6.11.1954
Record Defeat: 0-8 v Arsenal, First Division 25.2.1933
Record Cup Victory: 11-0 v Rossendale, FA Cup First Round 13.10.1884
Most League Goals in a Season: 114 Second Division 1954-55
Most Individual League Goals in a Season: 43, by Ted Harper in 1954-55
Most League Goals in Aggregate: 168 by Simon Garner between 1978-1992
Most League Appearances: 596 by Derek Fazackerley between 1970-1986
Most Capped Player: Bob Crompton 41 caps for England
Record Transfer Out: Alan Shearer to Newcastle for £15 million
Record Transfer In: Chris Sutton from Norwich City for £5 million

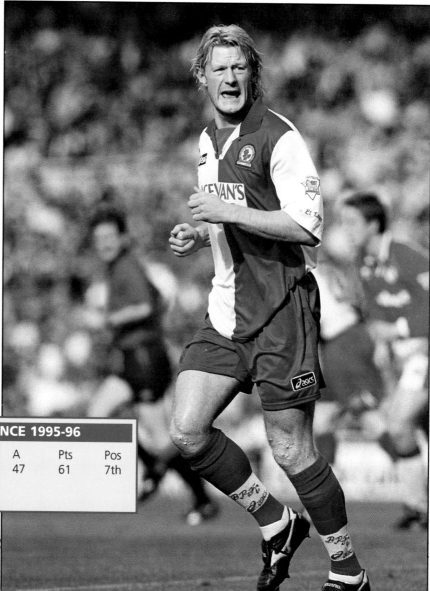

PREMIERSHIP PERFORMANCE 1995-96

P	W	D	L	F	A	Pts	Pos
38	18	7	13	61	47	61	7th

Top Scorer: Alan Shearer 31
Highest Attendance: 30,895 v Liverpool

CHELSEA

Address: Stamford Bridge, Fulham Road, London SW6 1HS
Telephone: 0171-385 5545
Ticket information: 0891 121011
Fax: 0171 381 4831
Current Ground Capacity: 44,000 (on completion of redevelopment)
Pitch Size: 113 x 74 yards
Chairman: Ken Bates
Managing Director: Colin Hutchinson
Match Secretary: Keith Lacy
Commercial Manager: Carole Phair
Youth Development Officers: D Collyer, B Dixson
Team Manager: Ruud Gullit
Assistant Manager: Gwyn Williams
First Team Coach: Graham Rix
Physio: Michael Banks
Reserve Coach: Mick McGiven
Nickname: The Blues
Team Colours: Blue shirts with yellow trim, blue shorts, white socks

Right: **Super Blue, Mark Hughes**
Main picture: **Ruud Gullit takes on Boro's Steve Vickers**

ROLL OF HONOUR

League Champions: 1954-55 (once)
FA Cup Winners: 1970 (once)
League Cup winners: 1965 (once)
Charity Shield Winners: 1955 (once)
European Cup-Winners' Cup Winners: 1971 (once)

OTHER RECORDS

Record Attendance: 82,905, v Arsenal First Division 12.10.1935
Record League Victory: 9-2 v Glossop NE, Second Division 1.9.1906
Record Defeat: 1-8 v Wolverhampton Wanderers, First Division 26.9.1953
Record Cup Victory: 13-0 v Jeueness Hautcharage, European Cup-Winners Cup First Round Second Leg 29.9.1971
Most League Goals in a Season: 98 Division One 1960-61
Most Individual League Goals in a Season: 41 by Jimmy Greaves in 1960-61
Most League Goals in Aggregate: 164 by Bobby Tambling between 1958-1970
Most League Appearances: 655 by Ron Harris between 1962-1980
Most Capped Player: Ray Wilkins 24 caps for England
Record Transfer Out: Gordon Durie to Tottenham Hotspur for £2.2 million
Record Transfer In: Franck Lebeouf from Strasbourg for £2.5 million

PREMIERSHIP PERFORMANCE 1995-96

P	W	L	D	F	A	Pts	Pos
38	12	14	12	46	44	50	11th

Top Scorer: John Spencer 13
Highest Attendance: 31,137 v Liverpool

COVENTRY CITY

Address: Highfield Road Stadium
King Richard Street, Coventry
CV2 4FW
Telephone: 01203 234000
Ticket information: 01203 234020
Fax: 01203 234099
Current Ground Capacity: 23,500
Pitch Size: 110 x 75 yards
Chairman: BA Richardson
Deputy Chairman: MC McGinnity
Secretary: Graham Hover
Sales & Marketing Manager:
Mark Jones
Team Manager: Ron Atkinson
Assistant Manager/Coach:
Gordon Strachan
Physio: George Dalton
Nickname: Sky Blues
Team Colours: Sky/navy stripes, navy
shorts and socks

ROLL OF HONOUR

FA Cup Winners: 1987 (once)

OTHER RECORDS

Record Attendance: 51,455 v
Wolves, Second Division 29.4.1967
Record League Victory: 9-0 v Bristol
City, Third Division (South) 28.4.1934
Record Defeat: 2-10 v Norwich City,
Third Division (South) 15.3.1930
Record Cup Victory: 7-0 v
Scunthorpe United, FA Cup First
Round 24.11.1934
Most League Goals in a Season:
108 Third Division (South) 1931-32
**Most Individual League Goals in a
Season:** 49 by Clarrie Bourton in
1931-32
Most League Goals in Aggregate:
171 by Clarrie Bourton between
1931-1937
Most League Appearances: 486 by
George Curtis between 1956-70
Most Capped Player: Dave
Clements, 21 caps for Northern
Ireland
Record Transfer Out: Phil Babb to
Liverpool for £3.6 million
Record Transfer In: Gary McAllister
from Leeds United for £3.3 million.

PREMIERSHIP PERFORMANCE 1995-96

P	W	D	L	F	A	Pts	Pos
38	8	14	16	42	60	38	16th

Top Scorer: Dion Dublin 14
Highest Attendance: 23,344 v Manchester United

The Sky Blues celebrate

DERBY COUNTY

Address: Baseball Ground, Shaftesbury Crescent, Derby DE3 8NB
Telephone: 01332 340505
Fax: 01332 293514
Current Ground Capacity: 18,000
Pitch Size: 110 x 71 yards
Chairman: LV Pickering
Vice-Chairman: PJ Gadsby
Chief Executive: Keith Loring
Secretary: Keith Pearson
Commercial Manager:
Colin Tunnicliffe
Team Manager: Jim Smith
Coaches: Steve Maclaren
Billy McEwan
Physio: Peter Melville, Gordon
Guthrie
Nickname: The Rams
Team Colours: White shirts, black
shorts, white socks

ROLL OF HONOUR

League Champions: 1971-72, 1974-75 (twice)
FA Cup Winners: 1946 (once)
Charity Shield Winners: 1975 (once)

OTHER RECORDS

Record Attendance: 41,826 v Tottenham Hotspur, First Division 20.9.1969
Record League Victory: 9-0 v Wolves, First Division 10.1.1891 & v Sheffield W, First Division 21.1.1899
Record Defeat: 2-11 v Everton, FA Cup First Round 18.1.1890
Record Cup Victory: 12-0 v Finn Harps, UEFA Cup First Round, first leg 15.9.1976
Most League Goals in a Season: 111, Third Division (North), 1956-57
Most Individual League Goals in a Season: 37 by Jack Bowers in 1930-31 & by Ray Straw in 1956-57
Most League Goals in Aggregate: 292 by Steve Bloomer between 1892-1906 & 1910-14
Most League Appearances: 486 by Kevin Hector between 1966-78 & 1980-82
Most Capped Player: Peter Shilton 34 caps for England
Record Transfer Out: Dean Saunders to Liverpool for for £2.9 million
Record Transfer In: Craig Short from Notts County for £2.5 million

Super Rams Ron Willems and
Inset picture: **Dean Sturridge**

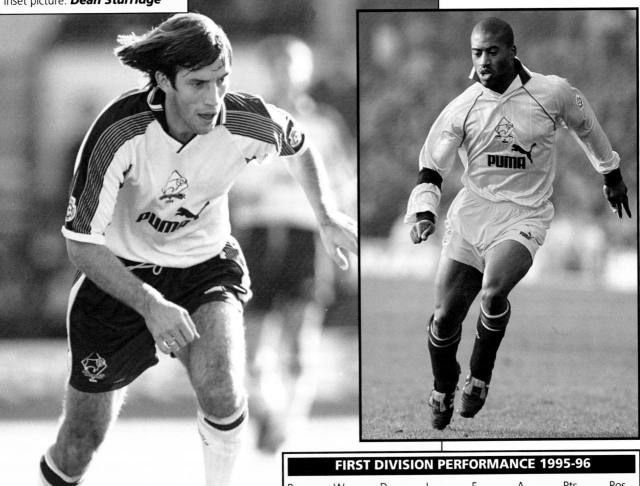

FIRST DIVISION PERFORMANCE 1995-96

P	W	D	L	F	A	Pts	Pos
46	21	16	8	69	48	79	2nd

Top Scorer: Dean Sturridge 20
Highest Attendance: 17,460 v Wolves

EVERTON

Address: Goodison Park,
Liverpool L4 4EL
Telephone: 0151-330 2200
Ticket information: 0891 121599
Fax: 0151-286 9114
Current Ground Capacity: 40,200
Pitch Size: 112 x 78 yards
Chairman: Peter R Johnson
Secretary: Michael J Dunford
Commercial Manager:
Andrew Watson
Youth Development Officer: R Hall
Team Manager: Joe Royle
**Assistant Manager/First Team
Coach:** Willie Donachie
Reserve Team Coach: Jimmy Gabriel
Physio: Les Helm
Nickname: The Toffees
Team Colours: Blue shirts, white
shorts, blue/black socks

Andrei Kanchelskis on the ball

ROLL OF HONOUR

League Champions: 1890-91, 1914-15, 1927-28, 1931-32, 1938-39, 1962-63, 1969-70, 1984-85, 1986-87 (9 times)
FA Cup Winners: 1906, 1933, 1966, 1984, 1995 (5 times)
Charity Shield Winners: 1928, 1932, 1963, 1970, 1984, 1985, 1986-shared, 1987, 1995 (9 times)
European Cup-Winners' Cup Winners: 1985 (once)

OTHER RECORDS

Record Attendance: 78,299 v Liverpool, First Division 18.9.1948
Record League Victory: 9-1 v Manchester City, First Division 3.9.1906
Record Defeat: 4-10 v Tottenham Hotspur, First Division 11.10.1958
Record Cup Victory: 11-2 v Derby County FA Cup First Round 18.1.1890
Most League Goals in a Season: 121 Second Division, 1930-31
Most Individual League Goals in a Season: 60* by Dixie Dean in 1927-28
Most League Goals in Aggregate: 349 by Dixie Dean between 1925-1937
Most League Appearances: 532, by Neville Southall between 1981-1996
Most Capped Player: Neville Southall 86 caps for Wales
Record Transfer Out: Gary Lineker to Barcelona for £2.75 million
Record Transfer In: Andrei Kanchelskis from Manchester United for £5.5 million
*All-time league record

PREMIERSHIP PERFORMANCE 1995-96

P	W	D	L	F	A	Pts	Pos
38	17	10	11	64	44	61	6th

Top Scorer: Andrei Kanchelskis 16
Highest Attendance: 40,127 v Aston Villa

LEEDS UNITED

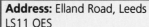

Address: Elland Road, Leeds
LS11 OES
Telephone: 0113 2716037
Ticket information: 0113 710710
Fax: 0113 2720370
Current Ground Capacity: 40,000
Pitch Size: 117 x 72 yards
President: The Rt Hon The Earl of
Harewood LLD
Chairman: W. Fotherby
Vice-Chairman: PJ Gilman
Secretary: Nigel Pleasants
Commercial Manager: Bob Baldwin
Youth Development Officer:
J Bilton
Team Manager: Howard Wilkinson
Assistant Manager: Mick Hennigan
Coaches: Paul Hart, Eddie Gray, David
Williams, Robin Wray
Physios: Geoff Ladley, Alan Sutton
Nickname: United
Team Colours: All white with
yellow/blue trim

ROLL OF HONOUR

League Champions: 1968-69 1973-74, 1991-92 (3 times)
FA Cup Winners: 1972 (once)
League Cup winners: 1968 (once)
Charity Shield Winners: 1969, 1992 (twice)
UEFA Cup Winners: 1968, 1971 (twice)

OTHER RECORDS

Record Attendance: 57,892 v Sunderland, FA Cup Fifth Round replay 15.3.1967
Record League Victory: 8-0 v Leicester City, First Division 7.4.1934
Record Defeat: 1-8 v Stoke City, First Division 27.8.1934
Record Cup Victory: 10-0 v Lyn (Norway), European Cup First Round first leg
17.9.1969
Most League Goals in a Season: 98 Second Division 1927-28
Most Individual League Goals in a Season: 42 by John Charles in 1953-54
Most League Goals in Aggregate: 168 by Peter Lorimer between 1965-1979
and 1983-1986
Most League Appearances: 629 by Jack Charlton between 1953-1973
Most Capped Player: Billy Bremner 54 caps for Scotland
Record Transfer Out: Gary Speed to Everton for £3.5 million
Record Transfer In: Tomas Brolin from Parma for £4.5 million

PREMIERSHIP PERFORMANCE 1995-96

P	W	D	L	F	A	Pts	Pos
38	12	7	19	40	57	43	13th

Top Scorer: Tony Yeboah 12
Highest Attendance: 39,801 v Manchester United

Tony Yeboah, about to strike!

LEICESTER CITY

Address: City Stadium, Filbert Street, Leicester LE2 7FL
Telephone: 0116 2915000
Ticket information: 0116 2915232
Fax: 0116 2470585
Current Ground Capacity: 22,517
Pitch Size: 112 x 75 yards
Chairman: Tom Smeaton
Vice-Chairman: John Elsom FCA
Chief Executive: Barry Pierpoint
Football Secretary: Ian Silvester
Company Secretary: Steve Kind
Team Manager: Martin O'Neill
Physio: Alan Smith
Nickname: The Filberts
Team Colours: All blue

ROLL OF HONOUR

League Cup winners: 1964 (once)

OTHER RECORDS

Record Attendance: 47,298 v Spurs, FA Cup Fifth Round 18.2.1928
Record League Victory: 10-0 v Portsmouth, First Division 20.10.1938
Record Defeat: 0-12 v Nottingham Forest, First Division 21.4.1909
Record Cup Victory: 8-1 v Coventry City League Cup Fifth Round 1.12.1964
Most League Goals in a Season: 109 Second Division 1956-57
Most League Goals in a Season: 44 by Arthur Rowley in 1956-57
Most Individual League Goals in Aggregate: 259 by Arthur Chandler between 1923-35
Most League Appearances: 528 by Adam Black between 1920-35
Most Capped Player: John O'Neill 29 caps for Northern Ireland
Record Transfer Out: Mark Draper to Aston Villa for £3.25 million
Record Transfer In: Mark Draper from Notts County for £1.25 million

FIRST DIVISION PERFORMANCE 1995-96

P	W	D	L	F	A	Pts	Pos
46	19	14	13	66	60	71	5th*

*Promoted via play-offs
Top Scorer: Iwan Roberts 19
Highest Attendance: 20,911 v Derby County

LIVERPOOL

Address: Anfield Road, Liverpool
L4 OTH
Telephone: 0151-263 2361
Ticket information: 0151-260 9999
Fax: 0151-260 8813
Current Ground Capacity: 41,000
Pitch Size: 110 x 74 yards
Chairman: DR Moores
Chief Executive/General Secretary:
Peter B Robinson
Commercial Manager: Mike Turner
Director of Youth:
Steve Heighway
Team Manager: Roy Evans
Assistant Manager: Doug Livermore
Coach: Ronnie Moran
Physio: Mark Leather
Nickname: The Pool
Team Colours: All red

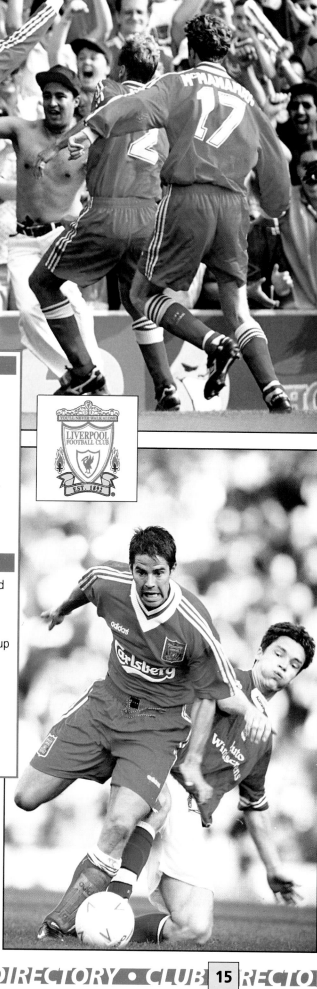

ROLL OF HONOUR

League Champions: 1900-01, 1905-06, 1921-22, 1922-23, 1946-47, 1963-64, 1965-66, 1972-73, 1975-76, 1976-77, 1978-79, 1979-80, 1981-82, 1982-83, 1983-84, 1985-86, 1987-88, 1989-90 (18 times)
FA Cup Winners: 1965, 1974, 1986, 1989, 1992 (5 times)
FA Cup & League 'Double' Achieved: 1985-86 (once)
League Cup winners: 1981, 1982, 1983, 1984, 1995 (5 times)
Charity Shield Winners: 1964-shared, 1965-shared, 1966, 1974, 1976, 1977-shared, 1979, 1980, 1982, 1986-shared, 1988, 1989, 1990 (13 times)
European Cup Winners: 1977, 1978, 1981, 1984 (4 times)
UEFA Cup Winners: 1973, 1976 (twice)
European Super Cup Winners: 1977 (once)

OTHER RECORDS

Record Attendance: 61,905 v Wolverhampton Wanderers, FA Cup Fourth Round 2.2.1952
Record League Victory: 10-1 v Rotherham Town, Second Division 18.2.1896
Record Defeat: 1-9 v Birmingham City, Second Division 11.12.1954
Record Cup Victory: 11-0 v Stromsgodset Drammen, European Cup-Winners' Cup First Round first leg 17.9.1974
Most League Goals in a Season: 106, Second Division 1895-96
Most Individual League Goals in a Season: 41 by Roger Hunt in 1961-62
Most League Goals in Aggregate: 245 by Roger Hunt between 1959-1969
Most League Appearances: 640 by Ian Callaghan between 1960-1978
Most Capped Player: Ian Rush 73 caps for Wales
Record Transfer Out: Ian Rush to Juventus for £2.75 million
Record Transfer In: Stan Collymore from Nottingham Forest for £8.5 million

PREMIERSHIP PERFORMANCE 1995-96

P	W	D	L	F	A	Pts	Pos
38	20	11	7	70	34	71	3rd

Top Scorer: Robbie Fowler 28
Highest Attendance: 40,820 v Chelsea

Above: *Stan Collymore celebrates his first goal for The Reds!*
Right: *Jamie Redknapp on the attack*

1995-96 DIARY OF A SEASON

SATURDAY 13th

In time honoured fashion the Charity Shield match is played at Wembley and sees 1994-95 FA Cup winners Everton beating Champions Blackburn 1-0. The only goal of the game is scored by Vinny Samways - a brilliant lob over the head of Tim Flowers.

SATURDAY 19th

The FA Premier League season begins in the middle of one of the hottest summers on record – and the football is every bit as scorching! Liverpool's new boy Stan Collymore lives up to his expensive price tag by scoring the only goal of the game against Sheffield Wednesday at Anfield–from all of 25-yards. It's a strange day for Matt Le Tissier who scores a hat-trick for Southampton, yet sees his side lose 4-3 to Nottingham Forest at The Dell. Aston Villa serve up an opening day lesson for Manchester United at Villa Park, by winning 3-1. Reigning champions Blackburn get off to a solid start thanks to a 1-0 home victory over QPR – Alan Shearer is the scorer. Rob Lee, Peter Beardsley and Les Ferdinand score one each as Newcastle trounce Coventry 3-0 at St James' Park. West Ham lose 2-1 at home to Leeds for whom Tony Yeboah scores twice. New boys Bolton get their Premiership baptism with a 3-2 defeat at Wimbledon.

SUNDAY 20th

Middlesbrough new boy Nick Barmby steals the show at Highbury, scoring the first goal. Ian Wright equalises for Arsenal a few minutes later – but big summer buys David Platt and Dennis Bergkamp hardly get a look in.

MONDAY 21st

Tony Yeboah volleys home the only goal of the game as Leeds beat Liverpool at Elland Road. Tony's fabulous shot is already being hailed as a potential 'Goal of the Season' contender!

TUESDAY 22nd

The Magpies are looking good – French ace David Ginola is in fantastic form and Les Ferdinand scores twice as Newcastle beat Bolton 3-1 at Burnden Park. Rob Lee adds a third, and Gudni Bergsson replies for Wanderers.

Above: *Wednesday's Mark Pembridge beats Liverpool's Jamie Redknapp to the ball*

Below left: *Double Dutch as Southampton's Ken Monkou challenges Forest's Bryan Roy*

Below: *Nick Barmby celebrates his strike for Boro against the Gunners*

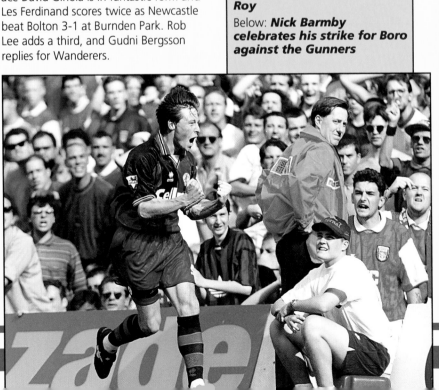

WEDNESDAY 23rd
Paul Telfer and Dion Dublin both score for Coventry in a 2-1 win over Manchester City at Highfield Road – Uwe Rosler replies for City. Wimbledon take advantage of poor defensive work by QPR, to win 3-0 at Loftus Road – Oyvind Leonhardsen, Dean Holdsworth and Jon Goodman are the scorers. Blackburn go down 2-1 at Sheffield Wednesday. Villa keep up their good start with a 1-0 away win at Tottenham. Manchester United record their first victory of the season, 2-1 at home to West Ham.

SATURDAY 26th
Middlesbrough's first ever Premiership match at their new Riverside Stadium sees them beat Chelsea 2-0 with goals from Craig Hignett and Jan-Aage Fjortoft. Blackburn lose again, this time by a 2-1 scoreline to Bolton at Burnden Park; Wanderers put up an an excellent defensive display. Everton beat Southampton 2-0 at Goodison Park. Aston Villa come unstuck at Leeds, losing 2-0 to goals from Gary Speed and David White. Wimbledon lose for the first time in the campaign - 3-1 away to Manchester United. Roy Keane scores twice, with United's other goal coming from Andy Cole. Robbie Earle replies for the Dons. Liverpool trounce Spurs 3-1 at White Hart Lane - John Barnes hits two, Robbie Fowler one. Manchester City lose their third game in a row, 1-0 to QPR at Loftus Road.

SUNDAY 27th
Kevin Keegan's Newcastle show their class again in a 2-0 away win over Sheffield Wednesday. David Ginola scores his first goal in England, and Peter Beardsley rounds off the afternoon with his second of the season.

MONDAY 28th
In the battle of last season's giants Blackburn lose 2-1 at home to Manchester United. Lee Sharpe and David Beckham are on target for the Red Devils, while Alan Shearer replies for Rovers.

TUESDAY 29th
Nottingham Forest's Kevin Campbell scores against his old club Arsenal in a 1-1 draw at Highbury. David Platt had struck first for the Gunners.

WEDNESDAY 30th
A night for drawing. Chelsea and Coventry 2-2 at Stamford Bridge; Southampton and Leeds 1-1 at The Dell; West Ham and Spurs 1-1 at Upton Park and Wimbledon and Sheffield

Wednesday 2-2 at Selhurst Park. Elsewhere, Neil Ruddock scores the only goal of the game as Liverpool beat QPR at Anfield; Villa win 1-0 at home against Bolton; and Everton add to Manchester City's problems with a 2-0 victory at Maine Road. Meanwhile, Newcastle march onwards with a 1-0 defeat of Middlesbrough at St James' Park. August ends with Newcastle in top spot with a maximum 12 points, two ahead

of Leeds. At the foot of the table sit Southampton and Manchester City with just a single point each.

Above: *Spurs' 'keeper Ian Walker punches clear against Liverpool*

Below: *Action from Middlesbrough's first League game down by the Riverside, against Chelsea*

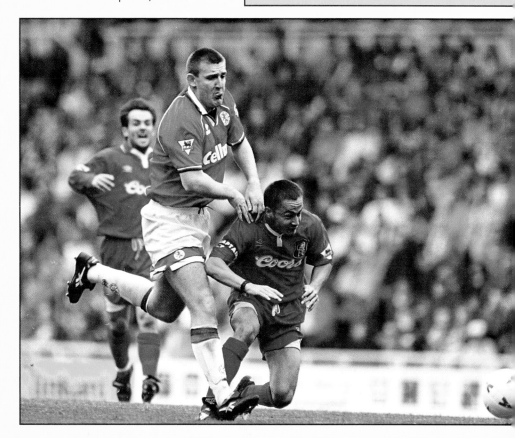

SATURDAY 9th

International action holds up the Premiership programme until the second Saturday in the month. Table-toppers Newcastle slip up with a 1-0 defeat by Southampton at The Dell. Jim Magilton scores from a perfectly placed Matt Le Tissier corner-kick. Leeds also lose, 2-1 away to Tottenham. Mark Bright scores twice as Sheffield Wednesday crush QPR 3-0 at Loftus Road, Wednesday's third goal comes from O'Neill Donaldson. Promoted sides Bolton and Middlesbrough share the points in a 1-1 draw at Burnden Park. Ryan Giggs scores Manchester United's winner in a 3-2 victory at Everton. Liverpool lose 1-0 to Wimbledon at Selhurst Park - Mick Harford scores the Dons' goal.

SUNDAY 10th

A last minute goal by Ian Wright piles even more pressure on luckless Manchester City as they go down 1-0 Arsenal at Maine Road.

MONDAY 11th

Chelsea's flying Dutchman Ruud Gullit is the star of the show as the Blues beat West Ham 3-1 at Upton Park. Two of Chelsea's goals come from John Spencer, the other from Dennis Wise. Don Hutchison replies for the Hammers.

TUESDAY 12th

Honours are even in a hard-fought 0-0 draw between Middlesbrough and Southampton at the Riverside Stadium.

SATURDAY 16th

Jamie Redknapp, Robbie Fowler and Stan Collymore are all on target as Liverpool beat Blackburn 3-0 at Anfield. Manchester United win 3-0 at home to Bolton with two goals from Paul Scholes, one from Ryan Giggs. Chelsea also record a 3-0 home victory, against Southampton - Frank Sinclair, Ruud Gullit and Mark Hughes are the scorers. At Highbury a solitary Ian Wright penalty gives Arsenal the points in the London derby against West Ham. Teddy Sheringham scores twice in Spurs' magnificent 3-1 away win at Sheffield Wednesday. The game's other goals were supplied by Wednesday players - Mark Bright, and Des Walker whose fluffed clearance ended up in his own net. QPR also record a fine 3-1 away victory at Leeds. Daniele Dichio hits two, Trevor Sinclair one - with United's reply coming from David Wetherall. Newcastle beat Manchester City 3-1 at St James' Park and remain top of the table.

SUNDAY 17th

Nottingham Forest maintain their unbeaten run with a 3-2 home win against Everton. Paul Rideout scores twice for the visitors, but an unfortunate own-goal by Dave Watson and further goals from Forest's Jason Lee and Ian Woan seal the points for the home side.

SATURDAY 23rd

A great day for strikers. Robbie Fowler scores four in Liverpool's 5-2 defeat of Bolton at Anfield. Tony Yeboah scores three for Leeds in a 4-2 away win at Wimbledon. Dennis Bergkamp hits two in Arsenal's 4-2 home win against Southampton. Julian Dicks continues the scoring theme by hitting both West Ham's goals from the penalty spot in a 2-1 home win against Everton. Elsewhere, Middlesbrough take the points with a 1-0 away win at Manchester City; Villa and Forest draw 1-1 at Villa Park while Sheffield Wednesday and Manchester United share the points in a goalless draw at Hillsborough.

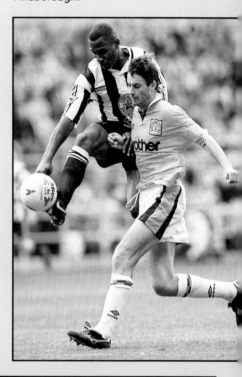

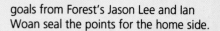

Left: *Intense concentration from Paul Scholes (Manchester United) and Barry Horne (Everton)*

Right: *Newcastle's Les Ferdinand gets to the ball ahead of Manchester City's Kit Symons*

Below: *Blackburn's Colin Hendry chases Jason McAteer at Anfield*

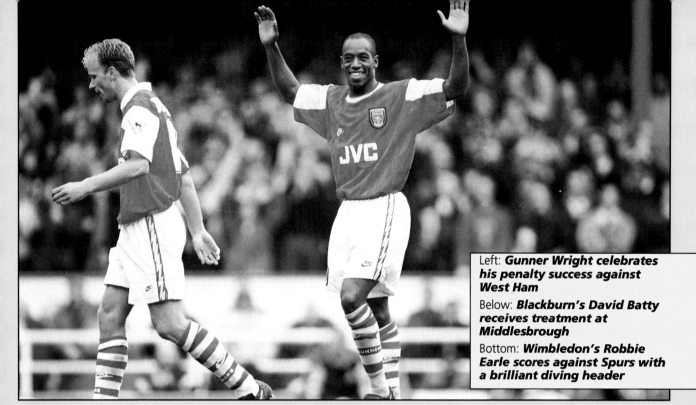

Left: **Gunner Wright celebrates his penalty success against West Ham**

Below: **Blackburn's David Batty receives treatment at Middlesbrough**

Bottom: **Wimbledon's Robbie Earle scores against Spurs with a brilliant diving header**

SUNDAY 24th

In form Les Ferdinand scores both Newcastle's goals in their 2-0 home win against Chelsea. The second goal is perhaps a little fortuitous - Les was struck by a Dimitri Kharine clearance and the ball rebounded into the net!

MONDAY 25th

QPR lead Tottenham 2-0 after 46 minutes of their encounter at Loftus Road. But Spurs claw their way back into the game and emerge as 3-2 victors. Rangers goals came from Daniele Dichio and Andy Impey, while Teddy Sheringham is twice on target for Spurs (one from the penalty spot). Jason Dozzell supplies the game's other goal.

SATURDAY 30th

Teddy Sheringham again scores twice, as Spurs beat Wimbledon 3-1 at White Hart Lane. A Mark Hughes goal earns Chelsea three points in the London derby against Arsenal at Stamford Bridge. Forest demolish Manchester City with a 3-0 scoreline at the City Ground – Jason Lee scores twice, Steve Stone once. Middlesbrough beat Blackburn 2-0 at The Riverside Stadium. Aston Villa destroy Coventry 3-0 at Highfield Road - Savo Milosevic scores twice for Villa. A brilliant Tony Yeboah goal opens the scoring for Leeds at home to Sheffield Wednesday, Gary Speed later adds a second. September ends with Newcastle still occupying top spot with 18 points – one ahead of Aston Villa. Manchester United, Leeds, Liverpool and Arsenal complete the top six placings. At the bottom Southampton, Bolton and Manchester City occupy the Drop Zone.

SEPTEMBER

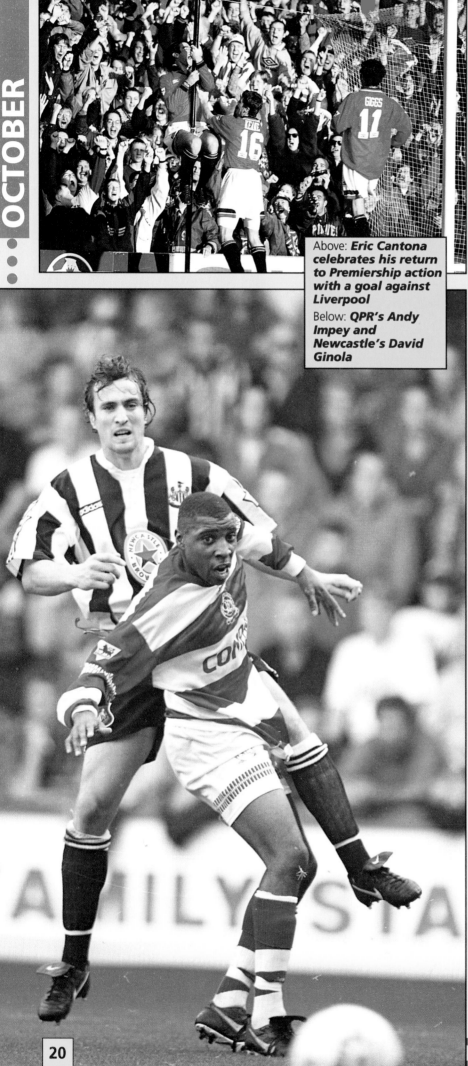

Above: *Eric Cantona celebrates his return to Premiership action with a goal against Liverpool*

Below: *QPR's Andy Impey and Newcastle's David Ginola*

SUNDAY 1st
October begins with two Super Sunday games in which Newcastle beat Everton 3-1 at Goodison Park; and Manchester United and Liverpool share the points in a 2-2 draw at Old Trafford. Newcastle's Les Ferdinand celebrates by scoring his 100th league goal, but the day's top scorer is Robbie Fowler who hits two goals for the Anfield Reds. The day also sees the return of Eric Cantona to first team action with Man United, following his long ban after the notorious incident at Selhurst Park in January - and he scores the equaliser from the penalty-spot.

MONDAY 2nd
Southampton and West Ham share the points in a goalless draw down at The Dell.

SATURDAY 14th
The Premier League programme resumes after a break for international action (England drew 0-0 with Norway). The Arsenal strike force - Merson, Bergkamp and Wright - all score as The Gunners lash Leeds 3-0 at Elland Road. Keith Gillespie scores twice in Newcastle's 3-2 away win at QPR. Rangers' Daniele Dichio also scores twice in the game. Dennis Wise scores the only goal of the game as Chelsea beat Aston Villa at Villa Park. Manchester United's Paul Scholes scores in their 1-0 derby win over City at Old Trafford. Lars Bohinen scores on his debut for Blackburn, in a 2-1 home win against Southampton.

MONDAY 16th
Tony Cottee scores his first Premier League goal in six months as West Ham beat Wimbledon 1-0 at Selhurst Park. It is the Hammers' first away win of the season.

SATURDAY 21st
Newcastle are the Premiership's top scorers of the day, with a 6-1 thrashing of Wimbledon at St James' Park - the tally includes a Les Ferdinand hat-trick. Paul Scholes is twice on target for Manchester United as they outclass Chelsea with a 4-1 scoreline at Stamford Bridge. A last minute equaliser by Alan Shearer saves the day for Blackburn at West Ham - Iain Dowie had opened the scoring for the Hammers. A last minute goal by Colin Cooper gives Forest a 3-2 home win against Bolton.

SUNDAY 22nd
Honours are even as Everton and Spurs draw 1-1 at Goodison Park. Down at The Dell Liverpool beat Southampton 3-1. Steve McManaman scores twice.

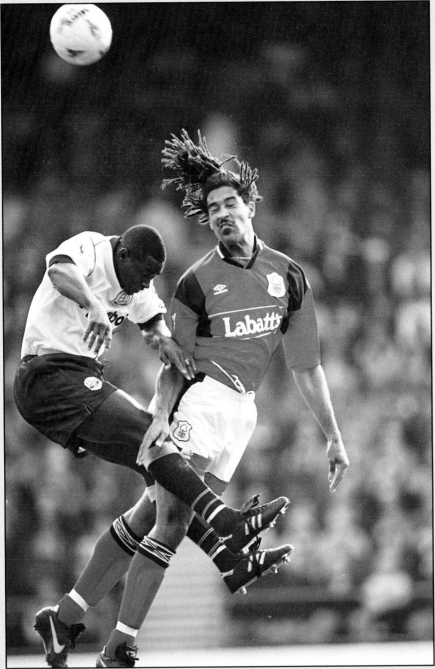

Left: *Wimbledon's Alan Reeves gets in a shot against Newcastle*

Below left: *Jason Lee of Forest and Chris Fairclough of Bolton in hair-raising action*

Below: *Spurs' Chris Armstrong goes flying against Everton*

SATURDAY 28th

Leeds skipper Gary McAllister hits a hat-trick as Leeds beat Coventry 3-1 at Elland Road. Ian Rush and Robbie Fowler both score twice as Liverpool thrash Manchester City 6-0 at Anfield - Jamie Redknapp and Neil Ruddock supply the other goals. Neil Shipperley also hits two as Southampton beat Wimbledon 2-1 at Selhurst Park. Blackburn hit top form as they chalk-up a 3-0 home win over Chelsea. Gary Pallister and Andy Cole are the target men as Manchester United beat Middlesbrough 2-0 at Old Trafford.

SUNDAY 29th

A David Ginola goal gives Newcastle a share of the points in a 1-1 draw at White Hart Lane - but Spurs' boss Gerry Francis is adamant that his side should have had two penalties.

MONDAY 30th

Bolton chalk-up only their second victory of the season, beating Arsenal 1-0 at Burnden Park. The goal is scored by John McGinlay.

OCTOBER

Above: *Ryan Giggs on a run against Arsenal*

Below: *David Hillier (Arsenal) and Sol Campbell (Spurs) in North London derby action*

SATURDAY 4th

Arsenal's Dennis Bergkamp is the hero of Highbury, scoring the only goal of a marvellous game against Manchester United. Coventry's troubles increase with a 3-2 home defeat by Spurs. Manchester City win the Drop Zone clash against Bolton, with Nicky Summerbee scoring the only goal of the game. Brazilian star Juninho makes his Premiership debut for Middlesbrough in a 1-1 draw with Leeds at The Riverside Stadium. Newcastle step up the pressure at the top with a 2-1 home win against Liverpool. Savo Milosevic scores twice in Aston Villa's 4-1 victory at West Ham.

SUNDAY 5th

Graham Stuart puts the finishing touch to a fine move involving Anders Limpar and Andrei Kanchelskis to ensure Everton of all three points against Blackburn at Goodison Park.

MONDAY 6th

Forest hammer Wimbledon 4-1 at The City Ground. The result marks the Dons' seventh consecutive Premier League defeat.

WEDNESDAY 8th

Robert Lee's goal settles the score at 1-0 to Newcastle in their home clash with Blackburn. It is United's first Premier League win against Rovers.

SATURDAY 18th

The Premier League campaign resumes after a break for international action. The big result of the day is Blackburn's 7-0 thrashing of Forest at Ewood Park. Alan Shearer hits a hat-trick, Lars Bohinen scores twice, while Mike Newell and Graeme Le Saux round up the scoreline with one each. To make matters worse for Forest Steve Chettle is sent-off. The scoreline represents Blackburn's highest ever score in the Premier League. Two goals by Andrei Kanchelskis set up Everton's 2-1 victory against Liverpool in the Merseyside derby at Anfield. Ryan Giggs also scores twice in Manchester United's 4-1 home win against Southampton. Giggs' first goal, after 16 seconds, is one of the quickest ever seen at Old Trafford. Spurs beat Arsenal 2-1 in the North London derby at White Hart Lane. Bolton are beaten 3-0 by West Ham at Burnden Park.

SUNDAY 19th

QPR and Coventry draw 1-1 at Loftus Road. Rangers score with a Simon Barker 25-yarder on 37 minutes. Coventry equalise through Dion Dublin 15 minutes from time.

MONDAY 20th

Tommy Johnson's 30th minute goal separates the sides in the Southampton v Aston Villa clash at The Dell. The Saints almost score on the stroke of half time, but Mark Bosnich scoops a Neil Shipperley effort off the line.

TUESDAY 21st

Despite being 2-1 down at one stage, Arsenal turn the tables to beat Sheffield Wednesday 4-2 at Highbury. Spurs destroy Middlesbrough's unbeaten home run, thanks to a disputed Chris Armstrong goal.

SATURDAY 25th

In the Drop Zone Coventry plunge into deeper trouble after a 3-2 home defeat by Wimbledon. Bolton lose 1-0 at Southampton, while Manchester City do themselves a huge favour with a 1-0 home win against Aston Villa. At the top of the table Newcastle increase the pressure with a 2-1 home win against Leeds. Both the Magpies goals, from Lee and Beardsley, come in the space of 70 seconds, to wipe out Brian Deane's earlier strike for Leeds. Middlesbrough record a fine 2-1 victory over Liverpool at The Riverside. Tony Cottee scores a late winner for West Ham in the London derby with QPR at Upton Park.

SUNDAY 26th

Arsenal and Blackburn play out a 0-0 draw at Highbury.

MONDAY 27th

An Eric Cantona penalty gives Manchester United an equaliser against Nottingham Forest at the City Ground. Paul McGregor had scored for Forest.

Top: *Chris Armstrong scores Spurs' winning goal against Arsenal*

Above: *Manchester United's Gary Neville challenges Southampton's Gordon Watson*

Below: *Tony Cottee hammers home West Ham's winner against QPR*

NOVEMBER

SATURDAY 2nd
Alan Shearer hits a superb hat-trick as Blackburn defeat West Ham 4-2 at Ewood Park. Manchester City win 1-0 at Leeds, the goal coming on the hour from Gerry Creaney. The points are shared in each of the days six other Premiership fixtures.

SUNDAY 3rd
Despite being behind twice, Wimbledon hold leaders Newcastle to a 3-3 draw at Selhurst Park. The Dons' Dean Holdsworth and the Magpies' Les Ferdinand both score twice in the match.

SATURDAY 9th
Coventry shock Blackburn with a magnificent 5-0 victory at Highfield Road. Middlesbrough record a 4-1 home win against Manchester City. Leaders Newcastle slip up with a 1-0 defeat by Chelsea at Stamford Bridge. The Blues goal comes from Dan Petrescu. Liverpool's Stan Collymore scores the only goal of the game against Bolton at Burnden Park. Teddy Sheringham's 14th goal of the season earns Spurs the points in a 1-0 defeat of QPR at White Hart Lane.

MONDAY 11th
West Ham's Ludek Miklosko is sent-off just before half time in the match against Everton at Goodison Park. Everton take full advantage to win 3-0.

SATURDAY 16th
Savo Milosevic hits a superb hat-trick in Aston Villa's 4-1 home defeat of Coventry. Graeme Le Saux is seriously injured in Blackburn's 1-0 defeat of Middlesbrough at Ewood Park. Marc Degryse scores twice at Hillsborough as Sheffield Wednesday win the Yorkshire derby against Leeds by a 3-2 margin. Bolton's woes increase with a 2-1 defeat at Queens Park Rangers. Chelsea hold Arsenal to a 1-1 draw at Highbury. Spurs win 1-0 at Wimbledon, thanks to a Ruel Fox goal five minutes from time. West Ham secure all three points as Iain Dowie makes it 2-1 against Southampton at Upton Park. Les Ferdinand is on target again as Newcastle get back on track with a 1-0 defeat of Everton at St James' Park.

SUNDAY 17th
Two goals by Robbie Fowler earn Liverpool a 2-0 victory over Manchester United at Anfield.

SATURDAY 23rd
Robbie Fowler is on top form again, scoring a hat-trick in Liverpool's 3-1 home win against Arsenal. Robert Lee scores twice as Newcastle continue to press their claim on the title with a 3-1 home win against Nottingham Forest. Brazilian star Juninho inspires Middlesbrough to a 4-2 victory over West Ham at The Riverside. Bolton claw back a 2-0 deficit to draw with Spurs in an absorbing game at White Hart Lane. Sheffield Wednesday and Southampton also draw 2-2, at Hillsborough. Manchester City are beaten 1-0 by Chelsea at Maine Road - their first home defeat in three months.

SUNDAY 24th
Christmas Eve brings an early present for Leeds, who dent Manchester

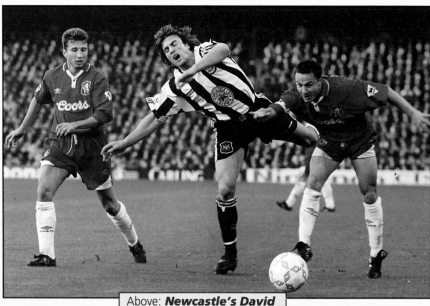

Above: *Newcastle's David Ginola gets Wised-up at Stamford Bridge*

Left: *Eric Cantona wriggles through against Chelsea in a 1-1 draw at Old Trafford*

Right: *Newcastle's Keith Gillespie has just scored against The Dons*

Above: **Tony Cottee (West Ham) and Ken Monkou (Southampton) go for the ball**
Below: **QPR celebrate Andy Impey's winner against Bolton**

United's title challenge with a 3-1 victory at Elland Road. Leeds' goals come from Gary McAllister, Tony Yeboah and Brian Deane. Andy Cole replies for the Red Devils.

TUESDAY 26th

Boxing Day action sees Paul Merson scoring twice in Arsenal's 3-0 home win against QPR. Everton's Graham Stuart is also on target twice in his club's 4-0 victory over Middlesbrough at Goodison Park. At Stamford Bridge Robbie Earle and Efan Ekoku wipe out an early goal by Dan Petrescu as Wimbledon beat Chelsea 2-1. David Batty has cause for celebration after scoring his first ever goal for Blackburn - it comes in a 2-0 win against Manchester City at Ewood Park. Alan Shearer scores Rovers other goal. A Jason Lee goal earns Forest a 1-0 home win against Sheffield Wednesday.

WEDNESDAY 27th

Manchester United demolish Newcastle with a fine 2-0 victory at Old Trafford - Andy Cole and Roy Keane are the scorers. The Magpies lead is now cut to 7 points. At the other of the table things worsen for Bolton with a 2-0 defeat by Leeds at Burnden Park. Tomas Brolin and David Wetherall score for Leeds.

SATURDAY 30th

Alan Shearer becomes the Premier League's first 'centurion' with his 100th goal in the competition. It comes in

Blackburn's 2-1 win over Spurs at Ewood Park. Robbie Earle scores twice in Wimbledon's 3-1 victory over Arsenal at Highbury. Andy Cole and Ryan Giggs are the target men as Manchester United enjoy a 2-1 home win against QPR. At the City Ground the Nottingham Forest v Middlesbrough game is settled 1-0 in Forest's favour with a Stuart Pearce penalty. An unfortunate own-goal by David Wetherall contributes to Everton's 2-0 win against Leeds at Goodison Park - Andrei Kanchelskis scores the Toffees' second. Two goals apiece for Chelsea's John Spencer and Liverpool's Steve

McManaman serve up an entertaining draw at Stamford Bridge. Bolton's worries increase with another defeat, this time by Coventry who win 2-1 at Burnden Park.

1995 closes with Newcastle sitting on top of the Premiership table with 45 points, ahead of Manchester United, Liverpool and Spurs. The relegation zone places are occupied by QPR, Manchester City and Bolton Wanderers. But the race is only half run yet - and there's loads more excitement to come...

PREMIER LEAGUE SCRAPBOOK

Top: **Young Gunners' fans meet their new hero Dennis Bergkamp**

Above: **Chelsea's John Spencer can't believe he's missed. Everton's Earl Barrett and Neville Southall are delighted that he has!**

Right: **Hammers' fans—forever blowing bubbles!**

THE F.A. PREMIER LEAGUE

Left: **Newcastle's Peter Beardsley gets a lift out of scoring!**

Bottom: **It's all smiles on the Blackburn bench!**

Below: **Southampton 'keeper Dave Beasant does a one man haka!**

27

1995-96 DIARY OF A SEASON

MONDAY 1st

New Year's Day action sees Spurs thrash Manchester United 4-1 at White Hart Lane–Chris Armstrong scores twice in the match. Robbie Fowler hit two as Liverpool beat Nottingham Forest 4-2 at Anfield. Sheffield Wednesday's Darco Kovacevic and David Hirst both hit two in their side's 4-2 home win against Bolton. Niall Quinn hits two for Manchester City as they beat West Ham 2-1 at Maine Road – and to complete the set Duncan Ferguson gets two in Everton's 3-2 away win at Wimbledon.

TUESDAY 2nd

Roy McFarland loses his job as manager of Bolton, leaving Colin Todd in charge at Burnden Park. Newcastle win again at St James' Park–2-0 against Arsenal - David Ginola opens the scoring in the first minute of the first half, while Les Ferdinand scores in the first minute of the second half. The Magpies are 7 points ahead of Manchester United at the top of the table. A last minute goal by Paul Furlong earns Chelsea a 2-1 victory against QPR at Loftus Road - Rangers slide to 19th position.

SATURDAY 13th

Desperate for points, Bolton are on the winning end of a 1-0 result at home to Wimbledon, thanks to a John McGinlay penalty in the 44th minute. Tomas Brolin scores both goals in Leeds' 2-0 home win against West Ham. Paul Merson, David Platt and Glen Helder all score in Arsenal's 3-2 victory at Middlesbrough. Alan Shearer increases QPR's worries by scoring the only goal of the game as Blackburn win at Loftus Road. Mark Hughes is sent-off as Chelsea draw 1-1 with Everton at Goodison Park.

SUNDAY 14th

A 44th minute slip-up by Coventry's John Salako allows Newcastle's Steve Watson to score the only goal of the game at Highfield Road. The Magpies appear to be marching towards the title.

SATURDAY 20th

In the top club v bottom club clash at St James' Park, Newcastle beat Bolton 2-1. The Magpies' goals come from Paul Kitson and Peter Beardsley - his 100th league goal for Newcastle. Bolton's reply comes from Gudni Bergsson. Liverpool smash Leeds 5-0 at Anfield - Neil Ruddock and Robbie Fowler both score twice. The Reds' other goal is hit by Stan Collymore. Blackburn dominate Sheffield Wednesday to win 3-0 at Ewood Park. Arsenal lose 2-1 at home to Everton.

SUNDAY 21st

Aston Villa beat Spurs 2-1 at Villa Park. Paul McGrath opens the scoring in the 23rd minute. Ruel Fox equalises for Spurs three minutes later. Dwight Yorke gets the winner with a 20-yard drive 11 minutes from time.

MONDAY 22nd

Manchester United inflict a 1-0 defeat on West Ham at Upton Park- Eric Cantona scores from a Ryan Giggs pass on 8 minutes. The result marks the Hammers sixth defeat in seven games and keeps Manchester United in touch with leaders Newcastle.

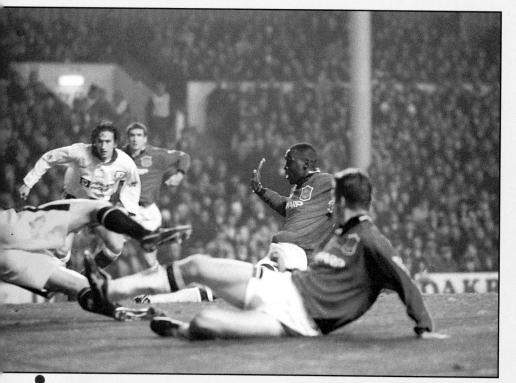

Above left: **Andy Cole scores for Manchester United against Spurs**

Left: **Drama from Chris Armstrong (Spurs) and Gary Neville (Manchester United)**

Right: *Action from Liverpool's 5-0 drubbing of Leeds*

Below: *Coventry v Newcastle - Watson v Salako*

Below right: *David Ginola opens the scoring for Newcastle against Arsenal*

Bottom right: *Stan Collymore's shot beats the Villa wall*

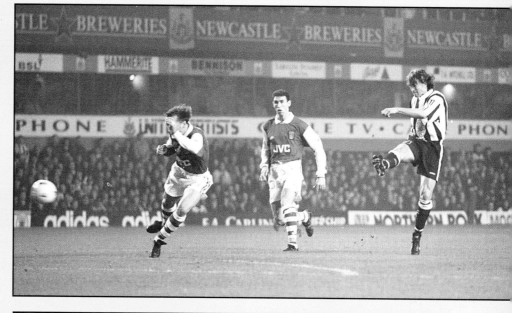

WEDNESDAY 31st

Down in the Drop Zone, Coventry put up a magnificent comeback to erase West Ham's 2-0 lead at Upton Park- but the Hammers grab the points with an Iain Dowie winner in the 85th minute. A Bryan Roy penalty earns Forest a 2-1 home win against Leeds. A goal each from Stan Collymore and Robbie Fowler give Liverpool a 2-0 victory at Aston Villa.

JANUARY

SATURDAY 3rd

Alan Shearer hits a magnificent hat-trick as Blackburn increase Bolton's worries with a 3-1 victory at Ewood Park. Eric Cantona scores twice (including a penalty) in Manchester United's 4-2 defeat of Wimbledon at Selhurst Park. Dwight Yorke hits two for Aston Villa in their 3-0 home defeat of Leeds. Meanwhile, Newcastle press on with a 2-0 home win against Sheffield Wednesday - Les Ferdinand and Lee Clark are the men on target.

SUNDAY 4th

Chelsea put in a magnificent performance against Middlesbrough at Stamford Bridge to notch a 5-0 victory. Gavin Peacock hits a hat-trick, while John Spencer and Paul Furlong round off the scoreline - but Ruud Gullit is the outstanding player in the game.

SATURDAY 10th

After the euphoria of last Sunday's victory Chelsea are brought back to earth with a 1-0 defeat at Coventry. In the battle of the Premiership's only champions to date, Manchester United beat Blackburn 1-0 at Old Trafford. Meanwhile current table-toppers Newcastle take all three points with a 2-1 scoreline in the north-east clash with Middlesbrough at the Riverside Stadium. Bolton's gloom deepens with a 2-0 home defeat by Aston Villa - Dwight Yorke hits both goals. Everton increase Manchester City's worries with a 2-0 victory at Goodison Park - to make matters worse City also have a player sent-off. A Dennis Bergkamp goal on the hour gives Arsenal a 1-0 victory at Forest.

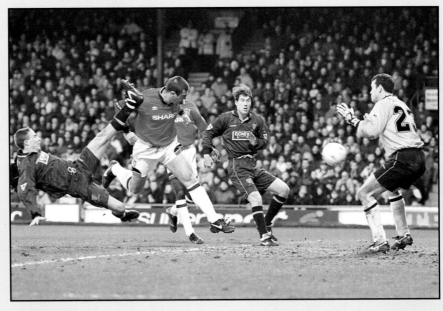

SUNDAY 11th

QPR slide deeper into trouble following their 2-1 home defeat by Liverpool. Mark Wright and Robbie Fowler are the on target men for the Reds. Daniele Dichio replies for Rangers.

SATURDAY 17th

QPR pick themselves up with a 3-1 away win at Sheffield Wednesday - Simon Barker scores twice in the match. Bottom club Bolton also hit top form with a stunning 4-1 away win at Middlesbrough. West Ham chalk-up their fourth successive Premiership victory with a 2-1 scoreline in the London derby against Chelsea.

WEDNESEDAY 21st

Watch out Newcastle! As the Magpies lose 2-0 at ever-improving West Ham, Manchester United lessen the gap at the top of the table with a 2-0 home win against Everton!

SATURDAY 24th

At Maine Road, Manchester City and Newcastle contest one of the best games of the season - it ends all-square at 3-3. The result helps City's cause, but dents the Magpies' title challenge. Liverpool win 3-2 at Blackburn, helped by perhaps the strangest goal of the season - Stan Collymore's 11th miniute shot hits a divot and spins past the bewildered Tim Flowers. Everton score three second half goals in eight minutes to beat Forest 3-0. Dennis Wise scores twice in Chelsea's 3-2 away win at Southampton. West Ham's luck runs out with a 1-0 home defeat by Arsenal.

SUNDAY 25th

Manchester United have a field day at Burnden Park, thrashing luckless Bolton 6-0 - Paul Scholes hits two of United's goals as they edge ever closer to Newcastle at the top. The gap is now down to 4 points. Wanderers will need a miracle if they are to survive the Big Drop.

WEDNESDAY 28th

Aston Villa new boy Julian Joachim scores in the 55th minute of his home debut against Blackburn. The game is wrapped up in Villa's favour with a Gareth Southgate goal in the 71st minute.

Above: *The Dons defence can't prevent Eric Cantona scoring for Manchester United*

Left: *Scott Green of Bolton chases Kevin Gallagher of Blackburn*

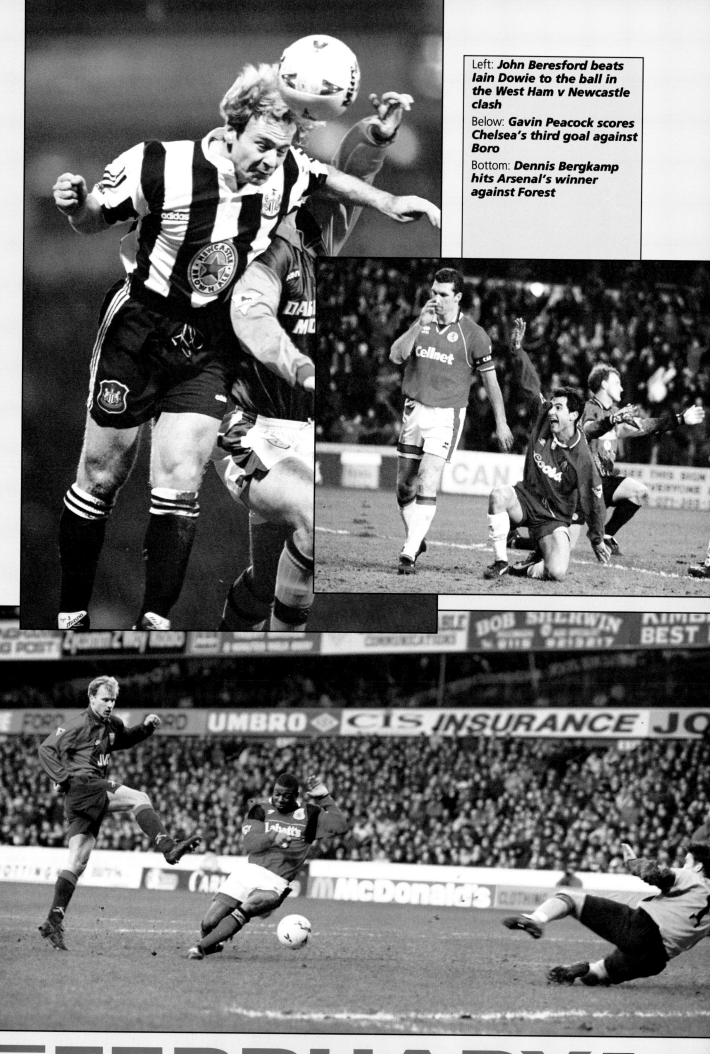

Left: *John Beresford beats Iain Dowie to the ball in the West Ham v Newcastle clash*

Below: *Gavin Peacock scores Chelsea's third goal against Boro*

Bottom: *Dennis Bergkamp hits Arsenal's winner against Forest*

FEBRUARY

SATURDAY 2nd

Blackburn's Alan Shearer notches his 31st goal in all competiotions as Rovers draw 1-1 with Manchester City at Maine Road. QPR and Arsenal share the points with a thrilling 1-1 draw at Loftus Road. Forest achieve their first away victory for four months with a 3-1 scoreline at Sheffield Wednesday. Brazilian star Branco makes his debut for Middlesbrough as a sub against Everton at The Riverside Stadium - Boro lose 2-0. A Jason Dozzell goal earns Spurs the points in a 1-0 home win against Southampton.

Top scorer Alan Shearer in action for Blackburn against Manchester City

SUNDAY 3rd

At Anfield, Liverpool put in a magnificent performance to beat Aston Villa 3-0. The goals all come within 8 minutes of kick-off - one from Steve McManaman, two from hot-shot Robbie Fowler. Villa were unable to recover. from such an explosive start.

MONDAY 4th

In the top of the table clash at St James' Park, Manchester United wrestle the initiative from Newcastle with a 1-0 victory. Eric Cantona scores the goal on 51 minutes, and the Magpies relinquish their 100% home record. The race for the Premier League title gets ever more interesting!

TUESDAY 5th

Manchester City goalkeeper Eike Immel plays brilliantly against Arsenal at Highbury. The Gunners bombard his goal throughout and could have had a hat-ful of goals - but Immel's form keeps the scoreline down to a respectable 1-3. John Hartson scores twice for Arsenal.

WEDNESDAY 6th

Savo Milosevic and Regi Blinker both score twice in the Villa v Wednesday clash at Villa Park - but Villa win thanks to Andy Townsend's 75th minute decider. QPR's misery continues with a 2-1 home defeat by Leeds. Tony Yeboah scores both of the visitors' goals.

SATURDAY 9th

QPR go down again, this time to a 4-2 scoreline at Aston Villa - Dwight Yorke scores twice for Villa. Coventry striker Noel Whelan suffers a gashed head in the 2-2 draw with Everton at Goodison Park - Duncan Ferguson scores both the Toffees' goals. Iain Dowie scores in the first minute of West Ham's home game against Middlesbrough. An hour later Julian Dicks adds to the Hammers' winning scoreline from the penalty spot.

TUESDAY 12th

Ruud Gullit and Nigel Clough score the goals in the 1-1 draw between Chelsea and Manchester City at Stamford Bridge.

WEDNESDAY 13th

Liverpool and Wimbledon share the points in a 2-2 draw at Anfield. Liverpool also have two 'goals' disallowed and the Dons almost snatch a winner late in the game. At Ewood Park Blackburn beat Leeds 1-0 with a Graham Fenton goal.

SATURDAY 16th

Super striker Alan Shearer hits a hat-trick in Blackburn's 3-2 away win at Tottenham. Bolton chalk-up a third successive away win, beating Coventry 2-0 and improve their survival chances - Alan Stubbs scores both Wanderers' goals. Liverpool keep up their Championship challenge with a 2-0 home win against Chelsea. Two goals - including one incredible strike - by Gheorghe Kinkladze give Manchester City a 2-1 home win against Southampton. A last minute goal by Eric Cantona rescues Manchester United in their 1-1 draw at QPR.

SUNDAY 17th

Honours are even in a 2-2 draw between Leeds and Everton at Elland Road. Brian Deane scores twice for United. Graham Stuart and Andrei Kanchelskis reply for the visitors.

MONDAY 18th

Newcastle get back on track with a thundering 3-0 dismissal of West Ham at St James' Park. The goals come from Philippe Albert, Faustino Asprilla (his first home goal for the Magpies) and Les Ferdinand.

WEDNESDAY 20th

Another Eric Cantona goal keeps Manchester United in the title race by securing a 1-0 home win against Arsenal. Bolton's worries return with a 3-2 home defeat by Spurs.

SATURDAY 23rd

Disaster for Newcastle as they go down 2-0 at Arsenal, allowing Manchester United to ease into top spot on goal difference (and without even playing!). Meanwhile, a Steve Stone goal gives Forest a 1-0 home win at the City Ground against title outsiders Liverpool. Bolton continue to battle it out in the Drop Zone, beating Sheffield Wednesday 2-1 at Burnden Park and lifting themselves off bottom spot in the process. QPR draw 1-1 at Chelsea, but slip to bottom of the table. Wimbledon perform heroically to beat Everton 4-2 at Goodison Park. The Dons' last two goals come in the last 5 minutes. Iain Dowie score twice as West Ham beat Manchester City 4-2 at Upton Park.

SUNDAY 24th

An Eric Cantona goal gives Manchester United a 1-0 victory over Spurs at Old Trafford and a three points lead at the top of the table. Newcastle's Les Ferdinand is named PFA Player of the Year. Liverpool's Robbie Fowler is named PFA Young Player of the Year for the second season in succession.

MONDAY 25th

Southampton take all three points with a 1-0 home win against fellow strugglers Coventry, thanks largely to a Man-of-the-Match performance by 'keeper Dave Beasant.

SATURDAY 30th

Relegation threatened QPR improve their chances of survival with a 3-0 home win against Southampton. The result marks only Rangers' second victory since Christmas. Andrei Kanchelskis scores twice in Everton's sensational 3-0 victory at Blackburn. Rovers' new-boy Garry Flitcroft is sent-off after just three minutes. Two second-half goals in the space of a minute contribute to Spurs' 3-1 home win over relegation threatened Coventry.

Top: *It's a tough Premiership debut for Branco, Boro's latest Brazilian signing*

Centre: *West Ham's Tim Braecker attempts to break through the Boro defence*

Above: *Spurs v Southampton – Dave Beasant turns Ruel Fox's shot wide*

WEDNESDAY 3rd

Liverpool and Newcastle play out a Premiership classic at Anfield - a game full of drama and spectacular action. The Reds have the edge as Robbie Fowler and Stan Collymore score two goals each - Stan getting the winner in the last minute. Les Ferdinand, David Ginola and Faustino Asprilla reply for the Magpies. The 4-3 scoreline keeps Liverpool in with a shout of the title, and dents Newcastle's ambitions. At Elland Road Leeds increase Southampton's worries with a 1-0 victory.

SATURDAY 6th

After their stirring midweek win Liverpool slip up with a 1-0 defeat at Coventry. Manchester United continue to press their claim at the top by winning the Manchester derby 3-2 at Maine Road. Newcastle pick themselves up with a 2-1 away win at struggling QPR. Peter Beardsley scores twice for the Magpies. Southampton beat Blackburn 1-0 at The Dell, thanks to a Matt Le Tissier penalty. Bottom of the table Bolton lose 3-0 at Everton.

MONDAY 8th

Newcastle's title ambitions take another bashing with a 2-1 defeat at Blackburn. The winning goal is scored by Geordie-born Graham Fenton with four minute to go. Meanwhile, Manchester United beat Coventry 1-0. Liverpool get back on track with a 2-0 home win against West Ham. Bolton's hopes brighten with a 2-1 home win against Chelsea.

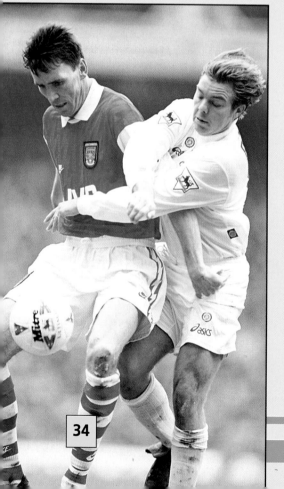

Southampton are back in trouble after a 3-0 drubbing at Aston Villa.

SATURDAY 13th

A grey day for Manchester United. They change their rather dull second strip at half time in the match against Southampton at The Dell - but not the outcome of the match. The Saints win 3-1. Blackburn thrash Forest 5-1 at The City Ground - Jason Wilcox scores twice for Rovers. Mark Hughes hits a hat-trick in Chelsea's 4-1 drubbing of Leeds at Stamford Bridge. In the relegation battle at Highfield Road, Coventry take the points with a 1-0 win over QPR. Bolton plunge deeper in to despair after a 1-0 defeat at West Ham.

SUNDAY 14th

Newcastle's title hopes are revived with a 1-0 home win against Aston Villa. Les Ferdinand gets the vital goal on 64 minutes.

Top: **QPR's Rufus Brevett chases Faustino Asprilla of Newcastle**

Above: **Boro's Nigel Pearson forces a way through the `Liverpool defence**

Left: **Action from Arsenal's 2-1 victory over Leeds**

MONDAY 15th

Arsenal and Spurs play out a 0-0 draw in the north-London derby at Highbury.

TUESDAY 16th

Robbie Fowler's 36th goal of the season in all competitions for Liverpool, equalises an earlier Andrei Kanchelskis strike for Everton to ensure a share of the spoils for both clubs in the Merseyside derby at Goodison Park.

WEDNESDAY 17th

Manchester United keep up the pressure at the top with a 1-0 win at Leeds. Roy Keane gets the vital goal. Newcastle keep pace with a 1-0 home win against

Above: **Coventry's keeper Steve Ogrizovic makes a brave dive as Manchester United's Andy Cole moves in**

Right: **Eion Jess (Coventry) and Alan Kimble (Wimbledon) in a chase for the ball**

struggling Southampton. Robert Lee gets the vital goal. Alan Shearer scores twice in Blackburn's 3-2 home win against Wimbledon, taking his tally to 30 Premiership goals this season.

WEDNESDAY 24th
Nine Premiership stars are in action for England against Croatia at Wembley in the build-up to Euro '96. The match is drawn 0-0.

SATURDAY 27th
The exciting Premier League programme resumes, but with neither of the top two teams in action. Third placed Liverpool beat Middlesbrough 1-0 with a Stan Collymore goal at Anfield. Sheffield Wednesday are in grave danger after their 5-2 thrashing by Everton at Hillsborough – Andrei Kanchelskis hits a hat-trick for the Merseysiders. Coventry help their cause with a fine 2-0 win at Wimbledon. Manchester City's hopes rise with a 1-0 win at Aston Villa. Southampton take all three points in the relegation battle against Bolton at Burnden Park. Bolton are now relegated, as are QPR. Despite Rangers' excellent 3-0 victory over West

Ham at Loftus Road, other results conspired against them. Any one of the five teams Manchester City, Southampton, Coventry, Sheffield Wednesday or Wimbledon –will occupy the third relegation spot.

SUNDAY 28th
The biggest Premiership's crowd of the season, 53,926, watch Manchester United's final home game a 5-0 win against Nottingham Forest. The goals

come from Paul Scholes, David Beckham (2), Ryan Giggs and Eric Cantona. United are now most definitely in the driving seat. Newcastle have it all to do.

MONDAY 29th
Newcastle are still in with a chance of winning the title after their 1-0 victory against Leeds at Elland Road. The goal scored by Keith Gillespie on 17 minutes keeps them in touch with leaders Manchester United.

APRIL

WEDNESDAY 1st

Liverpool and Arsenal draw 0-0 at Highbury. The Gunners attack for most of the match, but the Liverpool defence puts in some solid work with 'keeper David James playing a blinder.

TUESDAY 2nd

Newcastle's title challenge is dented in a 1-1 draw at Nottingham Forest. Peter Beardsley opens the scoring with a brilliant individual goal in the 32nd minute. But the lead is cancelled out by Ian Woan's wonderful 30-yard shot on 75 minutes. Spurs put on a fine display to defeat Leeds 3-1 at Elland Road. A back to his best Darren Anderton scores twice in the match.

SUNDAY 5th

The last day of the Premiership season. Arsenal defeat already relegated Bolton 2-1 at Highbury, while doomed QPR lose 3-0 at Forest. Manchester City fill the third relegation spot, despite a fine second half fightback in a 2-2 draw with Liverpool at Maine Road. City have the worse goal-difference of the three teams on 38 points - Coventry survive after a 0-0 draw at home to Leeds, while Southampton also secure their

Above: *Les Ferdinand has just equalised against Spurs - but it isn't enough*

Below: *Ryan Giggs fires home Manchester United's last Premiership goal of the season*

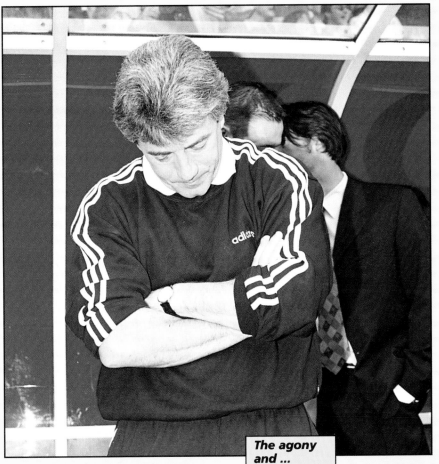

Premiership future with a 0-0 scoreline at home to Wimbledon.

Elsewhere, Blackburn beat Chelsea 3-2 at Stamford Bridge, Everton win 1-0 at home to Villa and the points are shared at Upton Park as West Ham and Wednesday draw 1-1.

In the day's two Championship deciders Newcastle are held 1-1 at St James' Park by Spurs. Jason Dozzell opens the scoring in the 57th minute. Les Ferdinand equalises for the Magpies with 19 mnutes left to play. But Newcastle are unable to find that all-important winner. They finish the season with feelings of great disappointment after a magnificent campaign that leaves them as runners-up on 78 points.

Meanwhile, a few miles south, at Middlebrough's Riverside Stadium, Manchester United take the FA Premier League title in flamboyant fashion. David May heads home a Ryan Giggs corner on 15 minutes. A Giggs corner leads to the second goal scored by Andy Cole in the 54th minute - and Ryan wraps things up at 3-0 with a brilliant 25-yard strike of his own ten minutes from time.

The agony and ... the ecstasy!

★★★★★ JUST CHAMPION!

That's all you can say about Manchester United. They are the Premier League's premier club, having won the title in three of the four seasons of its existence.

Here are some more brilliant pictures of the day when United collected their third Premier League Championship.

Left: *Eric Cantona lifts the FA Premier League trophy*

Below: *David May heads home Manchester United's first goal against Middlesbrough*

Opposite top: *United players celebrate their second goal against Boro, scored by Andy Cole*

Opposite bottom: *Steve Bruce and Alex Ferguson congratulate Roy Keane and Andy Cole*

MANCHESTER UNITED

FA Premier League Champions
1992-93, 1993-94, 1995-96

FA PREMIER LEAGUE
FACTS & FIGURES 1995-96

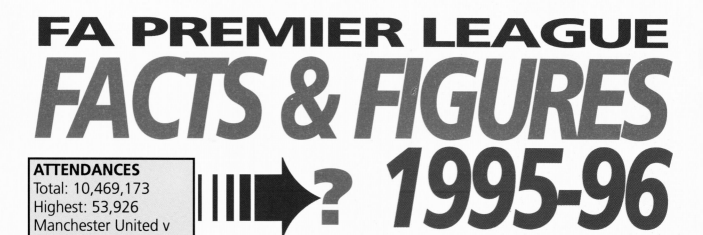

ATTENDANCES
Total: 10,469,173
Highest: 53,926
Manchester United v
Nottingham Forest

BIGGEST VICTORIES
Blackburn 7, Forest 0
Liverpool 6, Manchester City 0
Bolton W 0, Manchester United 6

MOST GOAL SCORED
73 by Manchester United

MOST GOALS IN A MATCH
8 – Sheffield W 6, Leeds United 2

LEAST GOALS SCORED
33 by Manchester City

FASTEST GOAL
Dwight Yorke, in 13 seconds, for
Aston Villa v Coventry City

		P	W	D	L	F	A	Pts
1	**Manchester United**	38	25	7	6	73	35	82

Another magnificent season for Alex Ferguson's team who rounded up a great title race with an FA Cup final victory over Liverpool to become the first club ever to win the 'double' twice'.

| 2 | **Newcastle United** | 38 | 24 | 6 | 8 | 66 | 37 | 78 |

Kevin Keegan's Magpies played some magnificent, entertaining football to lead the table nearly all the way, but they were pipped in the finishing straight by Man United.

| 3 | **Liverpool** | 38 | 20 | 11 | 7 | 70 | 34 | 71 |

A fine team that's starting to look like the Liverpool of old. It can't be long before another trophy arrives at Anfield. Losing FA Cup finalists to Manchester United

| 4 | **Aston Villa** | 38 | 18 | 9 | 11 | 52 | 35 | 63 |

Villa won the first domestic cup of the season - beating Leeds United 3-0 in the Coca-Cola Cup final. Looked to be serious title contenders for a while.

| 5 | **Arsenal** | 38 | 17 | 12 | 9 | 49 | 32 | 63 |

Big signings David Platt and Dennis Bergkamp helped the Gunners to an improved placing in '95-96. They had the Premiership's meanest defence and finished as London's top club.

| 6 | **Everton** | 38 | 17 | 10 | 11 | 64 | 44 | 61 |

It was much better showing in the Premier League for Joe Royle's side in 1995-96. Between October and April they climbed ten places.

| 7 | **Blackburn Rovers** | 38 | 18 | 7 | 13 | 61 | 47 | 61 |

The 1995 Champions began slowly, but recovered to climb the table in the second half of the '95-96 season. Sensational Alan Shearer was again the League's top scorer, with 31 goals.

| 8 | **Tottenham Hotspur** | 38 | 16 | 13 | 9 | 50 | 38 | 61 |

In mid-season Spurs were right up there battling for top spot. They were playing some fine, fluid football, but the challenge faded later in the campaign.

| 9 | **Nottingham Forest** | 38 | 15 | 13 | 10 | 50 | 54 | 58 |

A mid-table campaign for Frank Clark's Forest. They were England's most successful club in Europe, having reached the UEFA Cup quarter-finals.

| 10 | **West Ham United** | 38 | 14 | 9 | 15 | 43 | 52 | 51 |

The Hammers struggled at the wrong end of the table at the start of the season, but gradually pulled themselves up the ladder.

| 11 | **Chelsea** | 38 | 12 | 14 | 12 | 46 | 44 | 50 |

The signing of Dutch star Ruud Gullit inspired some fine performances for the Blues, but their challenge never really got under way. FA Cup semi-finalists.

| 12 | **Middlesbrough** | 38 | 11 | 10 | 17 | 35 | 50 | 43 |

A consistent spell took Bryan Robson's 'Boro up to sixth place in October and November. But their challenge faded away dramatically after Christmas.

| 13 | **Leeds United** | 38 | 12 | 7 | 19 | 40 | 57 | 43 |

Leeds began really well, and were occupying second spot at the end of August. Then came a gradual slide to thirteenth place. Losing finalists in the Coca-Cola Cup.

| 14 | **Wimbledon** | 38 | 10 | 11 | 17 | 55 | 70 | 41 |

Still going strong, although they finished five places lower than in 1994-95. The Dons pulled themselves out of trouble as the season came to a close.

| 15 | **Sheffield Wednesday** | 38 | 10 | 10 | 18 | 48 | 61 | 40 |

David Pleat's side never climbed above twelfth place all season. Their big moment of glory came in December with a marvellous 6-2 victory over Yorkshire rivals Leeds.

| 16 | **Coventry City** | 38 | 8 | 14 | 16 | 42 | 60 | 38 |

Coventry almost slipped out of the top flight for the first time in 29 years, but managed a last gasp escape!

| 17 | **Southampton** | 38 | 9 | 11 | 18 | 34 | 52 | 38 |

Dave Merrington's Saints struggled throughout the season and only avoided the drop on the last day of the campaign.

RELEGATED

| 18 | **Manchester City** | 38 | 9 | 11 | 18 | 33 | 58 | 38 |

Despite all Alan Ball's efforts, City never climbed above 17th position and were always among the candidates for the drop. They were also the Premiership's lowest scorers.

| 19 | **Queens Park Rangers** | 38 | 9 | 6 | 23 | 38 | 57 | 33 |

Having sold Les Ferdinand to Newcastle, goals seemed hard to come by for Rangers - and this ultimately led to the big drop

| 20 | **Bolton Wanderers** | 38 | 8 | 5 | 25 | 39 | 71 | 29 |

Poor Bolton struggled right from the start of the season. And, despite some stirring performances, survival was beyond them.

PREMIERSHIP STARS OF THE SEASON

DAVID GINOLA

David is the Premier League's best French import since Eric Cantona. The footballer with the film-star looks, was signed from Paris Saint-Germain by Kevin Keegan's Newcastle. His breathtaking wing play has been a delight to watch.

RUUD GULLIT

The presence of the Dutch master transformed Chelsea into a super side during 1995-96. He is a class act – whether playing at sweeper, in midfield or in attack. Blues' boss Glenn Hoddle must be credited with snapping-up such a great player on a free transfer. Ruud has now taken over as Chelsea's player/manager.

LES FERDINAND
Les is the latest in a long line of great Number Nines at St James' Park. Last season he led the line as the great north-east club occupied top spot for so long. He finished the campaign with 25 Premiership goals to his name, and he was voted PFA Players' Player of the Year.

DAVID JAMES
David's outstanding, acrobatic form between the posts for Liverpool throughout 1995-96 helped keep the Anfield club in touch with Manchester United and Newcastle at the top.

ROBBIE FOWLER
Liverpool's super striker continued to impress with his goal-getting prowess. For the second season in succession he finished as second top scorer, this time with 28 Premiership goals. His tip-top form won him a call-up to the England squad, and earned him the prestigious PFA Young Player of the Year Award for the second year running.

STEVE McMANAMAN
As each season goes by Liverpool's midfield master grows in stature. His new roving role in the Reds line-up perfectly suits his style of play. To see him running at an opposing defence is one of the Premier League's great sights!

TREVOR SINCLAIR
The fine form of Trevor Sinclair really stood out in 1995-96, despite the fact that his club, Queens Park Rangers, was struggling in the thick of the relegation battle for most of the campaign and were eventually relegated.

ALAN SHEARER
In a rather disappointing campaign for 1994-95 Premier League Champions Blackburn, super striker Alan Shearer remained as consistent as ever, banging in 31 Premiership goals and finishing as the top scorer. Alan became the most expensive player in the world after his £15 million transfer to Newcastle.

ERIC CANTONA
After returning from that infamous ban imposed in 1994-95, Eric Cantona made a telling contribution to Manchester United's title challenge, and he scored some vital goals. He also scored the winner in the FA Cup final to give United the 'double-double'. And he was named the Football Writers' Footballer of the Year for 1996.

47

WELCOME TO THE PREMIERSHIP

Congratulations to Sunderland and Derby County who enter the Premiership as 1995-96 Division One Champions and runners-up respectively.

Peter Reid's Sunderland picked themselves up brilliantly after a rather indifferent start. By the end of September they were sixth in the First Division table and remained in contention for a play-off place right up until February when they eased into the automatic promotion berths. Eventually they took the title with 83 points, four ahead of Jim Smith's Derby.

County were a little slower in getting their act together. At the start of the campaign they were actually down in the Division One danger zone. But a remarkable recovery saw a steady rise to a mid table position in November, followed by a leap to the top of the table a month later. From then on they were favourites for promotion and eventually went up with 79 points .

The third promotion place went to Leicester City after a thrilling play-off final at Wembley against Crystal Palace. The game was won in the last-minute of extra time by a goal from Steve Claridge.

The F.A. Premier League welcomes all three clubs.

Garry Parker equalises from the penalty spot, for Leicester against Crystal Palace in the play-off final at Wembley

Above: *Leicester boss Martin O'Neill is delighted*

PLAY-OFF ACTION

Above: **Steve Claridge scores the dramatic last minute winner**

Below: **Leicester City have made it!**

TOP★TEN
GOALSCORERS

1	ALAN SHEARER (Blackburn Rovers)	31
2	ROBBIE FOWLER (Liverpool)	28
3	LES FERDINAND (Newcastle United)	25
4	DWIGHT YORKE (Aston Villa)	17
5=	TEDDY SHERINGHAM (Spurs)	16
5=	ANDREI KANCHELSKIS (Everton)	16
7	IAN WRIGHT (Arsenal)	15
8=	STAN COLLYMORE (Liverpool)	14
8=	DION DUBLIN (Coventry City)	14
8=	ERIC CANTONA (Mancherster United)	14

25 goals for Les Ferdinand

Chart-topper – Alan Shearer

Robbie Fowler – 28 goals

MANCHESTER UNITED

Intense concentration from United's Andy Cole and Ryan Giggs

ROLL OF HONOUR

League Champions: 1907-08, 1910-11, 1951-52, 1955-56, 1956-57, 1964-65, 1966-67, 1992-93, 1993-94 1995-96 (10 times)

FA Cup Winners: 1909, 1948, 1963, 1977, 1983, 1985, 1990, 1994, 1996 (9 times)

FA Cup & League 'Double' Achieved: 1993-94, 1995-96 (twice)

League Cup winners: 1992 (once)

Charity Shield Winners: 1908, 1911, 1952, 1956, 1957, 1965-shared, 1967-shared, 1977-shared, 1983, 1990-shared, 1993 1994 (12 times)

European Cup Winners: 1968 (once)

European Cup-Winners' Cup Winners: 1991 (once)

European Super Cup Winners: 1991 (once)

OTHER RECORDS

Stadium Record Attendance: 76,962 Grimsby v Wolverhampton Wanderers, FA Cup semi-final 25.3.1939;

Club Record Attendance: 70,504 v Aston Villa, First Division 27.12.1920

Record League Victory: 10-0 v Wolves, First Division 15.10.1892

Record Defeat: 0-7 v Blackburn Rovers, First Division 10.4.1926

Record Cup Victory: 10-0 v RSC Anderlecht, European Cup Preliminary Round second leg 26.9.1956

Most League Goals in a Season: 103 First Division 1956-57 and 1958-59

Most Individual League Goals in a Season: 32, by Dennis Viollet in 1959-60

Most League Goals in Aggregate: 199, by Bobby Charlton between 1956-1973

Most League Appearances: 606, by Bobby Charlton between 1956-1973

Most Capped Player: Bobby Charlton 106 caps for England

Record Transfer Out: Paul Ince to Inter Milan for £7 million

Record Transfer In: Andy Cole from Newcastle United for £6.25 million

Address: Sir Matt Busby Way, Old Trafford, Manchester M16 0RA
Telephone: 0161-872 1661
Ticket information: 0161-872 0199
Fax: 0161-876 5502

Current Ground Capacity: 55,300

Pitch Size: 116 x 76 yards

Chairman/Chief Executive: Martin Edwards

Secretary: Kenneth Merrett

Commercial Manager: Danny McGregor

Youth Development Officer: Dave Bushell

Team Manager: Alex Ferguson CBE

Assistant Manager: Brian Kidd

Nickname: The Red Devils

Team Colours: Red shirts, white shorts, black socks

PREMIERSHIP PERFORMANCE 1995-96

P	W	D	L	F	A	Pts	Pos
38	25	7	6	73	35	82	1st

Top Scorer: Eric Cantona 14

Highest Attendance: 53,926 v Nottingham Forest

MIDDLESBROUGH

Above: **Juninho – Boro's brilliant Brazilian shows off his skills**
Right: **Nick Barmby celebrates**

Address: Cellnet Riverside Stadium, Middlesbrough, Cleveland TS3 6RS
Telephone: 01642 227227
Fax: 01642 248450
Current Ground Capacity: 30,300
Pitch Size: 115 x 75 yards
Chairman: S Gibson
Chief Executive: Keith Lamb
Commercial Manager: Graham Fordy
Head of Commercial & Marketing: John Knox
Youth Development Officer: Ron Bone
Team Manager: Bryan Robson
Assistant Manager: Viv Anderson
Coach: John Pickering
Physio: Bob Ward
Nickname: Boro
Team Colours: Red shirts, white shorts, red/black socks

ROLL OF HONOUR

Anglo-Scottish Cup winners: 1976

OTHER RECORDS

Record Attendance: (at Riverside Stadium) : 30,011 v Newcastle United, Premier League 10.2.1996
Record League Victory: 9-0 v Brighton, Second Division 23.8.1958
Record Defeat: 0-9 v Blackburn Rovers, Second Division, 6.11.1954
Record Cup Victory: 9-3 v Goole Town, FA Cup First Round 9.1.1915
Most League Goals in a Season: 122, Second Division 1926-27
Most Individual League Goals in a Season: 59, by George Camsell in 1926-27
Most League Goals in Aggregate: 326, by George Camsell between 1925-1939
Most League Appearances: 563, by Tim Williamson between 1902-1923
Most Capped Player: Wilf Mannion 26 caps for England
Record Transfer Out: Gary Pallister to Manchester United for £2.3 million
Record Transfer In: Nick Barmby from Tottenham for £5.2 million

PREMIERSHIP PERFORMANCE 1995-96

P	W	D	L	F	A	Pts	Pos
38	11	10	17	35	50	43	12th

Top Scorer: Nick Barmby 7
Highest Attendance: 30,011 v Newcastle United

NEWCASTLE UNITED

Address: St James' Park,
Newcastle-upon-Tyne NE1 4ST
Telephone: 0191-201 8400
Ticket information: 0191-261 1571
Fax: 0191-201 8600
Current Ground Capacity: 36,610
Pitch Size: 110 x 73 yards
President: TL Bennett
Chairman: Sir John Hall
Vice-Chairman: WF Shepherd
Chief Executive: AO Fletcher
General Manager & Secretary:
R Cushing
Assistant Secretary: A Toward
Marketing Control: Trevor Garwood
Youth Development Officer:
J Murray
Team Manager: Kevin Keegan
Assistant Manager:
Terry McDermott
Coach: C McMenemy
Physios: Derek Wright, Paul Ferris
Nickname: The Magpies
Team Colours: Black and white
striped shirts, black shorts, black socks

Main picture: *The classy Robert Lee*
Below: *Warren Barton on the ball for the Magpies*

ROLL OF HONOUR

League Champions: 1904-05, 1906-07, 1908-09, 1926-27 (4 times)
FA Cup Winners: 1910, 1924, 1932, 1951 1952, 1955 (6 times)
Charity Shield Winners: 1909 (once)
UEFA Cup Winners: 1969 (once)

OTHER RECORDS

Record Attendance: 68,386 v Chelsea, First Division 3.9.1930
Record League Victory: 13-0 v Newport County Second Division 5.10.1946
Record Defeat: 0-9 v Burton Wanderers, Second Division 15.4.1895
Record Cup Victory: 9-0 v Southport FA Cup Fourth Round 1.2.1932
Most League Goals in a Season: 98, First Division 1951-52
Most Individual League Goals in a Season: 36 by Hughie Gallacher in 1926-27
Most League Goals in Aggregate: 178 by Jackie Milburn between 1946-1957
Most League Appearances: 432 by Jim Lawrence between 1904-1922
Most Capped Player: Alf McMichael 40 caps for Northern Ireland
Record Transfer Out: Andy Cole to Manchester United for £6.25 million
Record Transfer In: Alan Shearer from Blackburn for £15 million

PREMIERSHIP PERFORMANCE 1995-96

P	W	D	L	F	A	Pts	Pos
38	24	6	8	66	37	78	2nd

Top Scorer: Les Ferdinand 25
Highest Attendance: 36,589 v Tottenham Hotspur

NOTTINGHAM FOREST

Address: City Ground, Nottingham NG2 5FJ
Telephone: 0115 9526000
Ticket information: 0115 9526002
Fax: 0115 9526003
Current Ground Capacity: 30,539
Pitch Size: 115 x 78 yards
Chairman: Fred Reacher
Vice-Chairman: I Korn
Secretary: Paul White
Commercial Manager: David Pullan
Youth Development Officer:
M Raynor
Team Manager: Frank Clark
Assistant Manager: Alan Hill
Coach: Liam O'Kane
Physio: John Haselden
Nickname: Reds
Team Colours: Red shirts with black shoulders, white shorts, red socks

Right: *Kevin Campbell on the move*
Bottom: *Mark Crossley stands guard for Forest*

ROLL OF HONOUR

League Champions: 1977-78 (once)
FA Cup Winners: 1898, 1959 (twice)
League Cup winners: 1978, 1979, 1989, 1990 (4 times)
Charity Shield Winners: 1978 (once)
European Cup Winners: 1979, 1980 (twice)
European Super Cup Winners: 1980 (once)

OTHER RECORDS

Record Attendance: 49,946 v Manchester United, First Division 28.10.1967
Record League Victory: 12-0 v Leicester Fosse, First Division 12.4.1909
Record Defeat: 1-9 v Blackburn Rovers, Second Division 10.4.1937
Record Cup Victory: 14-0 v Clapton FA Cup First Round 17.1.1891
Most League Goals in a Season: 110, Third Division (South) 1950-51
Most Individual League Goals in a Season: 36 by Wally Ardron 1950-51
Most League Goals in Aggregate: 199 by Grenville Morris between 1898-1913
Most League Appearances: 614 by Bob McKinlay between 1951-1970
Most Capped Player: Stuart Pearce 68 caps for England
Record Transfer Out: Stan Collymore to Liverpool for £8.5 million
Record Transfer In: Bryan Roy from Foggia for £2.9 million

PREMIERSHIP PERFORMANCE 1995-96

P	W	D	L	F	A	Pts	Pos
38	15	13	10	50	54	58	9th

Top Scorers: Bryan Roy, Ian Woan, Jason Lee - 8
Highest Attendance: 29,263 v Manchester United

Address: Hillsborough, Sheffield
S6 1SW
Telephone: 0114 2212121
Ticket information: 0114 2212400
Fax: 0114 2212122
Current Ground Capacity: 39,359
Pitch Size: 115 x 77 yards
Chairman: DG Richards
Vice-Chairman: KT Addy
Secretary: Graham Mackrell FCCA
General Manager: Alan Blanshard ACIB
Commercial Manager: Sean O'Toole
Youth Development Officer:
C Baker
Team Manager: David Pleat
Assistant Manager: Peter Shreeves
Physio: David Galley
Nickname: The Owls
Team Colours: Blue and white striped shirts, blue short, blue socks

SHEFFIELD WEDNESDAY

ROLL OF HONOUR

League Champions: 1902-03, 1903-04, 1928-29, 1929-30 (4 times)
FA Cup Winners: 1896, 1907, 1935 (3 times)
League Cup winners: 1991 (once)
Charity Shield Winners: 1935 (once)

OTHER RECORDS

Record Attendance: 72,841 v Manchester City FA Cup Fifth Round 17.2.1934
Record League Victory: 9-1 v Birmingham City, First Division 13.12.1930
Record Defeat: 0-10 v Aston Villa First Division 5.10.1912
Record Cup Victory: 12-0 v Halliwell, FA Cup First Round 17.1.1891
Most League Goals in a Season: 106 Second Division 1958-59
Most Individual League Goals in a Season: 46 by Derek Dooley in 1951-52
Most League Goals in Aggregate: 199 by Andy Wilson between 1900-1920
Most League Appearances: 502 by Andy Wilson between 1900-1920
Most Capped Player: Nigel Worthington 50 caps for Northern Ireland
Record Transfer Out: Paul Warhurst to Blackburn Rovers for £2.65 million
Record Transfer In: Des Walker from Sampdoria for £2.75 million

Wednesday men Mark Degryse and Des Walker

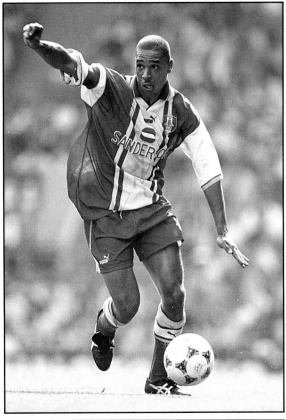

PREMIERSHIP PERFORMANCE 1995-96

P	W	D	L	F	A	Pts	Pos
38	10	10	18	48	61	40	15th

Top Scorer: David Hirst 13
Highest Attendance: 34,101 v Manchester United

SOUTHAMPTON

Address: The Dell, Milton Road,
Southampton SO15 2XW
Telephone: 01703 220505
Ticket information: 01703 228575
Fax: 01703 330360
Current Ground Capacity: 15,280
Pitch Size: 110 x 72 yards
Chairman: FGL Askham FCA
Vice-Chairman: K St. J Wiseman
Secretary: Brian Truscott
Team Manager: Graeme Souness
Assistant Manager: Phil Boersma
Physios: Don Taylor, Jim Joyce
Nickname: The Saints
Team Colours: Red and white striped
shirts, black shorts, red/white socks

ROLL OF HONOUR

FA Cup Winners: 1976 (once)

OTHER RECORDS

Record Attendance: 31,044 v
Manchester United, First Division
8.10.1969
Record League Victory: 9-3 v
Wolves, Second Division 18.9.1965
Record Defeat: 0-8 v Spurs, Second
Division 28.3.1936, and v Everton,
First Division 20.11.1971
Record Cup Victory: 7-1 v Ipswich
Town, FA Cup Third Round 7.1.1961
Most League Goals in a Season:
112 Third Division (South) 1957-58
**Most Individual League Goals in a
Season:** 39 by Derek Reeves in
1959-60
Most League Goals in Aggregate:
185 by Mick Channon between 1966-
67 & 1979-82
Most League Appearances: 713 by
Terry Paine between 1956-74
Most Capped Player: Peter Shilton
49 caps for England
Record Transfer Out: Alan Shearer
to Blackburn Rovers for £3.3 million
Record Transfer In: Neil Shipperley
from Chelsea for £1.2 million

Above: *Saint Matt Le Tissier*
Right: *Neil Shipperley playing against Spurs*

PREMIERSHIP PERFORMANCE 1995-96

P	W	D	L	F	A	Pts	Pos
38	9	11	18	34	52	38	17th

Top Scorer: Neil Shipperley, Matthew Le Tissier 7
Highest Attendance: 15,262 v Manchester United

SUNDERLAND

Address: Roker Park Ground, Sunderland SR6 9SW
Telephone: 0191 514 0332
Fax: 0191 514 5854
Current Ground Capacity: 22,657
Pitch Size: 113 x 74 yards
Chairman: JR Featherstone
Deputy-Chairman: GS Woods
General Manager/Secretary:
P Fiddaman BA (Hons) ACA
Commercial Manager: Alec King
Team Manager: Peter Reid
Coach: Paul Bracewell
Physio: Steve Smelt
Director of Youth: Jim Montgomery
Youth Coach: Ricky Sbragia
Nickname: Rokermen
Team Colours: Red and white striped shirts, black shorts, red/white socks

ROLL OF HONOUR

League Champions: 1891-92, 1892-93, 1894-95, 1901-02, 1912-13, 1935-36 (6 times)
FA Cup Winners: 1937, 1973 (twice)
Charity Shield Winners: 1936 (once)

OTHER RECORDS

Record Attendance: 75,118 v Derby County, FA Cup 6th Round replay 8.3.1933
Record League Victory: 9-1 v Newcastle Utd, First Division 5.12.1908
Record Defeat: 0-8 v West Ham United, First Division 19.10.1968
Record Cup Victory: 11-1 v Fairfield, FA Cup First Round 2.2.1895
Most League Goals in a Season: 109 First Division 1935-36
Most Individual League Goals in a Season: 43 by Dave Halliday 1928-29
Most League Goals in Aggregate: 209 by Charlie Buchan between 1911-1925
Most League Appearances: 537 by Jim Montgomery between 1962-1967
Most Capped Player: Martin Harvey 34 caps for Northern Ireland
Record Transfer Out: Marco Gabbiadini for £1.5 million to Crystal Palace
Record Transfer In: Don Goodman for £900,000 from West Bromwich Albion

Above: ***Top scorer Craig Russell***

Left: ***Steve Agnew salutes the Roker crowd***

FIRST DIVISION PERFORMANCE 1995-96

P	W	D	L	F	A	Pts	Pos
46	22	17	7	59	33	83	1st

Top Scorer: Craig Russell 13
Highest Attendance: 22,027 v West Bromwich Albion

TOTTENHAM HOTSPUR

Address: 748 High Road, Tottenham, London N17 0AP
Telephone: 0181-365 5000
Ticket information: 0181-365 5050
Fax: 0181-365 5005
Current Ground Capacity: 33,147
Pitch Size: 110 x 73 yards
Board of Directors - Executive
Chairman: AM Sugar
Chief Executive: CM Littner
Club President: WE Nicholson OBE
Club Secretary: Peter Barnes
Commercial Manager: Mike Rollo
Press Officer: John Fennelly
Team Manager: Gerry Francis
Assistant Manager: Roger Cross
Reserve Team Manager: Chris Hughton
Physios: Alasdair Beattie, Tony Lenaghan
Nickname: Spurs
Team Colours: White shirts, navy shorts, navy socks

ROLL OF HONOUR

League Champions: 1950-51, 1960-61 (twice)
FA Cup Winners: 1901, 1921, 1961, 1962, 1967, 1981, 1982, 1991 (8 times)
FA Cup & League 'Double' Achieved: 1960-61 (once)
League Cup winners: 1971, 1973 (twice)
Charity Shield Winners: 1920, 1951, 1961, 1962, 1967-shared, 1981-shared, 1991-shared (7 times)
European Cup-Winners' Cup Winners: 1963 (once)
UEFA Cup Winners: 1972, 1984 (twice)

OTHER RECORDS

Record Attendance: 75,038 v Sunderland, FA Cup Sixth Round 5.3.1938
Record League Victory: 9-0 v Bristol Rovers, Second Division 22.10.1977
Record Defeat: 0-7 v Liverpool, First Division 2.9.1978
Record Cup Victory: 13-2 v Crewe Alexandra, FA Cup Fourth Round replay 3.2.1960
Most League Goals in a Season: 115 First Division 1960-61
Most Individual League Goals in a Season: 37 by Jimmy Greaves 1962-63
Most League Goals in Aggregate: 220 by Jimmy Greaves between 1961-1970
Most League Appearances: 655 by Steve Perryman between 1969-1986
Most Capped Player: Pat Jennings 74 caps for Northern Ireland
Record Transfer Out: Paul Gascoigne to Lazio for £5.5 million
Record Transfer In: Chris Armstrong from Crystal Palace for £4.5 million

Main picture: *Teddy gets ready to shoot!*
Left: *Gary Mabbutt keeps Robbie Fowler at bay*

PREMIERSHIP PERFORMANCE 1995-96

P	W	D	L	F	A	Pts	Pos
38	16	13	9	50	38	61	8th

Top Scorer: Teddy Sheringham 16
Highest Attendance: 32,918 v Chelsea

WEST HAM UNITED

Main picture: **Danny Williamson sells a dummy**

Below: **Tony Cottee, Happy Hammer**

Address: Boleyn Ground, Green Street, Upton Park, London E13 9AZ
Telephone: 0181-548 2748
Ticket information: 0181-472 3322
Fax: 0181-548 2758
Current Ground Capacity: 25,982
Pitch Size: 112 x 72 yards
Chairman: TW Brown FCIS ATH, FCCA
Vice-Chairman: MW Cearnes ACIB
Secretary: Richard Skirrow
Youth Development Officer: J Hampson
Team Manager: Harry Redknapp
Assistant Manager: Frank Lampard
Coaches: Frank Burrows (1st teams), Tony Carr (Youth)
Physio: John Green Bsc (Hons) MCSP, SRP
Nickname: The Hammers
Team Colours: Claret shirts, white shorts, light blue socks

ROLL OF HONOUR

FA Cup Winners: 1964, 1975, 1980 (3 times)
Charity Shield Winners: 1964-shared (once)
European Cup-Winners' Cup Winners: 1965 (once)

OTHER RECORDS

Record Attendance: 42,322 V Tottenham Hotspur, First Division 17.10.1970
Record League Victory: 8-0 v Rotherham United, Second Division 8.3.1958
Record Defeat: 2-8 v Blackburn Rovers, First Division 26.12.1963
Record Cup Victory: 10-0 v Bury, League Cup Second Round, second leg 25.10 1983
Most League Goals in a Season: 101 Second Division 1957-58
Most Individual League Goals in a Season: 41 by Vic Watson in 1929-30
Most League Goals in Aggregate: 298 by Vic Watson between 1920-1935
Most League Appearances: 663 by Billy Bonds between 1967-1988
Most Capped Player: Bobby Moore 108 caps for England
Record Transfer Out: Tony Cottee to Everton for £2 million
Record Transfer In: Slaven Bilic from Karlsruhe for £1.65 million

PREMIERSHIP PERFORMANCE 1995-96

P	W	D	L	F	A	Pts	Pos
38	14	9	15	43	52	51	10th

Top Scorer: Julian Dicks 10, Tony Cottee 10
Highest Attendance: 24,324 v Liverpool

WIMBLEDON

Address: Selhurst Park, South Norwood, London SE25 6PY
Telephone: 0181-771 2233
Ticket information: 0181-771 8841
Fax: 0181-768 0640
Current Ground Capacity: 26,309
Pitch Size: 110 x 74 yards
Chairman: SG Reed
Vice-Chairman: J Lelliott
Owner/Managing Director: Sam Hammam
Chief Executive: David Barnard
Secretary: Steve Rooke
Marketing Manager: Sharon Sillitoe
Press Manager: Reg Davis
Team Manager: Joe Kinnear
Assistant Manager: Terry Burton
Physio: Steve Allen
Nickname: Crazy Gang
Team Colours: All blue with yellow trim

ROLL OF HONOUR

FA Cup Winners: 1988 (once)

OTHER RECORDS

Record Attendance: 25,432 v Manchester United, Premiership 9.5.1993
Record League Victory: 6-0 v Newport County, Third Division 3.9.1983
Record Defeat: 0-8 v Everton, League Cup Second Round 29.8.1978
Record Cup Victory: 7-2 v Windsor and Eton, FA Cup First Round 22.11.1980
Most League Goals in a Season: 97 Third Division 1983-84
Most Individual League Goals in a Season: 29 by Alan Cork in 1983-84
Most League Goals in Aggregate: 145 by Alan Cork between 1977-1992
Most League Appearances: 430 by Alan Cork between 1977-1972
Most Capped Player: Terry Phelan 8 caps for the Republic of Ireland
Record Transfer Out: Warren Barton to Newcastle United for £4 million
Record Transfer In: Efan Ekoku from Norwich City for £920,000

Above: **Efan Ekoku is challenged by Bolton's Gudni Bergsson**

Right: **Dean Holdsworth - a Don about to strike!**

PREMIERSHIP PERFORMANCE 1995-96

P	W	D	L	F	A	Pts	Pos
38	10	11	17	55	70	41	14th

Top Scorer: Robbie Earle 11
Highest Attendance: 25,423 v Manchester United

PREMIER LEAGUE
★★ COMPETITION ★★
17 GREAT PRIZES TO BE WON

Yes, we have SEVENTEEN superb prizes in this year's Premier League competition...

6 FIRST PRIZES of MITRE ULTIMAX FOOTBALLS!

5 SECOND PRIZES of Premier League SUBBUTEO GAMES from WADDINGTONS!

3 THIRD PRIZES of CORINTHIAN CARICATURE FIGURINES!

3 FOURTH PRIZES of COMPLETE MERLIN 1997 STICKER COLLECTIONS!

All you have to do is answer these two simple questions:

1. Which team scored the most Premier League goals in 1995-96?

2 Which team conceded the least Premier League goals in 1995-96?

Write your answers on a postcard or a sealed empty envelope, include your name, age and address and post to:

Premier League Competition
Grandreams Ltd
Jadwin House
205-211 Kentish Town Road
London NW5 2JU

Closing date for entries is 31st March 1997

A Mitre Ultimax Football will be awarded to the senders of the first six all correct entries drawn out of the bag on the closing date. Senders of the next five all correct entries drawn will each receive a Premier League Subbuteo game. Senders of the next three all correct entries drawn will each receive a set of Corinthian caricature figurines (one each of either Manchester United, England or Liverpool). Senders of the next three all correct entries drawn will each receive a complete Merlin 1997 Sticker Collection.
The publishers decision is final and no correspondence will be entered into.

From grass roots...

...Grow big shoots

Mitre

SOCCER RECORDS

LEAGUE CHAMPIONS

1888-89 Preston North End	1925-26 Huddersfield Town	1965-66 Liverpool
1889-90 Preston North End	1926-27 Newcastle United	1966-67 Manchester United
1890-91 Everton	1927-28 Everton	1967-68 Manchester City
1891-92 Sunderland	1928-29 Sheffield Wednesday	1968-69 Leeds United
1892-93 Sunderland	1929-30 Sheffield Wednesday	1969-70 Everton
1893-94 Aston Villa	1930-31 Arsenal	1970-71 Arsenal
1894-95 Sunderland	1931-32 Everton	1971-72 Derby County
1895-96 Aston Villa	1932-33 Arsenal	1972-73 Liverpool
1896-97 Aston Villa	1933-34 Arsenal	1973-74 Leeds United
1897-98 Sheffield United	1934-35 Arsenal	1974-75 Derby County
1898-99 Aston Villa	1935-36 Sunderland	1975-76 Liverpool
1899-1900 Aston Villa	1936-37 Manchester City	1976-77 Liverpool
1900-01 Liverpool	1937-38 Arsenal	1977-78 Nottingham Forest
1901-02 Sunderland	1938-39 Everton	1978-79 Liverpool
1902-03 The Wednesday	1939-46 competition suspended	1979-80 Liverpool
1903-04 The Wednesday	1946-47 Liverpool	1980-81 Aston Villa
1904-05 Newcastle United	1947-48 Arsenal	1981-82 Liverpool
1905-06 Liverpool	1948-49 Portsmouth	1982-83 Liverpool
1906-07 Newcastle United	1949-50 Portsmouth	1983-84 Liverpool
1907-08 Manchester United	1950-51 Tottenham Hotspur	1984-85 Everton
1908-09 Newcastle United	1951-52 Manchester United	1985-86 Liverpool
1909-10 Aston Villa	1952-53 Arsenal	1986-87 Everton
1910-11 Manchester United	1953-54 Wolverhampton Wanderers	1987-88 Liverpool
1911-12 Blackburn Rovers	1954-55 Chelsea	1988-89 Arsenal
1912-13 Sunderland	1955-56 Manchester United	1989-90 Liverpool
1913-14 Blackburn Rovers	1956-57 Manchester United	1990-91 Arsenal
1914-15 Everton	1957-58 Wolverhampton Wanderers	1991-92 Leeds United
1915-19 Competition suspended	1958-59 Wolverhampton Wanderers	
1919-20 West Bromwich Albion	1959-60 Burnley	**PREMIER LEAGUE**
1920-21 Burnley	1960-61 Tottenham Hotspur	
1921-22 Liverpool	1961-62 Ipswich Town	1992-93 Manchester United
1922-23 Liverpool	1962-63 Everton	1993-94 Manchester United
1923-24 Huddersfield Town	1963-64 Liverpool	1994-95 Blackburn Rovers
1924-25 Huddersfield Town	1964-65 Manchester United	1995-96 Manchester United

CHAMPIONSHIP WINS

18 – Liverpool
10 – Arsenal, Manchester United
9 – Everton
7 – Aston Villa
6 – Sunderland
4 – Newcastle United, Sheffield Wednesday
3 – Blackburn Rovers, Huddersfield Town, Leeds United,
      Wolverhampton Wanderers
2 – Burnley, Derby County, Manchester City, Portsmouth,
      Preston North End, Tottenham Hotspur
1 – Chelsea, Ipswich Town, Nottingham Forest, Sheffield United,
      West Bromwich Albion

THE F.A. PREMIER LEAGUE